LIVING
WITH
DYING

D0778421

LIVING WITH DYING

Glen W. Davidson

**RELIGION
AND
MEDICINE
SERIES**

Glen W. Davidson, Editor

AUGSBURG PUBLISHING HOUSE
MINNEAPOLIS, MINNESOTA

LIVING WITH DYING

In memory of the patients
who taught me
the meaning of
ars moriendi

Contents

A Letter
to the Reader

*For everything there is a season, and
a time for every matter under heaven:
A time to be born, and a time to die.*

ECCLES. 3:1 RSV

This book is about dying. It is also
about living. It is based on my re-
search from interviews with more than six hundred critically
and terminally ill patients, their families and friends, and
the health care personnel who served them. I have written
the book for relatives and friends of seriously ill patients to
help them better understand the emotional needs of their
loved one and respect their own feelings as well.

"What should I do?" "What is expected of me?" "Should
I be feeling this way?" These questions, and others, are
among the queries relatives and friends have when someone
dear to them is in health crisis.

Answers given in the book are tentative, though based on
empirical data. I assume that each of us has opinions about
how best to help a patient cope with dying. Yet, it is the patient who must finally judge which answers are appropriate to
questions generated by his crisis. The answers given here are

tentative, not only because there is still so much to learn, but because each patient has his own ways of handling crisis. Each patient exhibits any number of ambiguities, contradictions, and inconsistencies in coping with illness. It is difficult to say anything definitive without being confronted with contradictory data.

My efforts here are directed toward understanding the ways patients try to resolve the conflicts of their crises; therefore, my emphasis is on process. If you now relate to someone who is critically or terminally ill, you are part of his process in living with dying. How you relate to him will make a difference in how he copes. How you relate to him will also make a difference in how you cope.

I began following my curiosity concerning the ways human beings face mortality in 1960, in preparation for a dissertation which was called, *Basic Images of Death in America: An Historical Analysis.* I have learned much since that first attempt to interpret my findings. It was based on works of historians, religionists, and cultural analysts, but not those who were experiencing dying first hand. Nevertheless, I gained an abiding sense of how misleading generalizations and stereotypes about human behavior can be. Stereotypes, when used literally, convey notions of fixed behavior which are not confirmed by clinical evidence. But stereotypes can also be used as figurative description which permits us to make distinctions and identify unique beliefs and behavior. Since each of us has a unique history of experience, I intend to use stereotypes only in the latter sense. When I write that a majority of patients seemed to behave in some way or had a certain need, I hope you will take my statement as a guide by which you can better understand your loved one's uniqueness.

I conducted research at King's County Hospital, Brooklyn; the Stanford University Medical Center; and the University of Chicago Hospitals and Clinics. When my colleague, the late Carl Nighswonger, became director of the "Program on Death and Dying" at Chicago, I began correlating clinical data gathered there with cultural and sociological data. This book reflects my opinion that clinical data must be interpreted within the patient's context. A patient's needs in a major university teaching hospital may be different from the needs of a patient in a small community care-center. What is appropriate for helping someone from one culture may not be appropriate for a patient who has been reared in another culture. The principle is, the patient determines what is appropriate. For both relatives and health care staff, if we are to address the patient's needs, we must permit his feelings to take priority over our own.

My research has continued at the University of Iowa Hospitals and at the Memorial Medical Center and St. John's Hospital in Springfield, the two community hospitals that serve as teaching theaters for the Southern Illinois University School of Medicine.

This book is a development of thoughts expressed in a summer lecture at Mount Saint Vincent University, Halifax, and later in two lectures given at Saint Francis Xavier University, Antigonish, Nova Scotia. Contents of the book were tested at a Summer Institute on "Death and Human Experience" in 1973, organized by the Society for Religion in Higher Education and funded by The National Endowment for the Humanities. In between times, parts of it have been used in workshops throughout North America.

The manuscript has been constructively criticized by colleagues and friends, who, nevertheless, hold me entirely responsible for its contents. I must mention the assistance of Barbara Mowat of Auburn University, George Paterson of the University of Iowa, Fr. Don McNeill of Notre Dame University, Sr. Gerard Schweider of St. John's Hospital—

Springfield, and John Dawson of the Mountain States Tumor Institute. Mrs. Helen Melnyk knows the manuscript by heart after typing its many drafts. And Shirlee Proctor Davidson, R.N., knows not only what is included, but much other data that could not be included in a short book.

Fictitious names are used in the examples throughout the book, but all are illustrations of authentic clinical data.

Glen W. Davidson, Ph.D.
Associate Professor,
and Chief of Thanatology
Department of Psychiatry
Southern Illinois University
School of Medicine

LIVING
WITH
DYING

1

What Does Dying Mean?

*Ye shall not surely die: for God doth
know that in the day ye eat thereof,
then your eyes shall be opened, and
ye shall be as gods, knowing good
and evil.*

GENESIS 3:4-5 KJV

Dictionaries define "dying" as: "to
stop living," "to become dead." For
Bill Taylor, "dying" had been as remote as a dictionary
definition. It had, that is, until his physician told him just
how serious his health crisis was. Then he had to struggle
with what "dying" meant for him.

"Dying" is given any number of definitions, depending
on cultural, religious, and historical context. Definitions are
useful to help us clarify our understandings of life's phenomena. But understanding a phenomenon is not the same as
grasping its meaning. We can *understand* something without
any emotional involvement. But *meaning* connotes emotional
involvement, and no definition is real to us until it is tested
in our experiences of living.

When circumstances force us to reflect on what dying
means, we discover that our definition depends on what we

expect from life. Our expectations shape our behavior, beliefs, and values. What we expect life to be, and the meaning we attach to the ending of that life, define what dying means to us. Even if we have a fairly clear idea of what life means to us, most of us react with disbelief as did Bill, when we are surprised by a health crisis.

Bill was a fifty-year-old truck driver fighting a serious disease of the lungs. "When I came in here, I believed that I would never really die; I thought death is only an illusion. When I was told what I have, when I realized that I would die because of it, I felt like I had been hit by a Mack truck! I couldn't believe it. I couldn't talk about it. I wanted to, but I just couldn't find the right words. I didn't even know the right questions to ask. I guess I've lived as though things would always be the same."

Bill's expectations for living were, in one sense, uniquely his own. And out of his expectations, he had developed a fairly elaborate ethic about what is appropriate and what is offensive in his life. Initially, he judged his illness to be offensive and his suffering to be inappropriate. That meant that either he or someone else was at fault. In another sense, his expectations reflected the cultural, religious, sociological, and psychological contexts in which he lived.

At first, Bill was too startled by his health crisis to be very reflective about his expectations. But later, he became aware of, and confused by the contradiction between his expectations for unending life and the realities of his illness. Then the contradiction, not the illness, startled him. But as he worked through the contradiction in his mind, he began to adjust to living with illness, and life, for him, took on new meaning.

Like Bill, you may never have given much thought to your expectations for life. Dying, for you, may have been as remote as a dictionary definition—until health crisis startled you into reflecting about what life really means to you. If so, it is important to understand that your expectations for life do not need to be consistent, rational, and orderly. Few people are so rigid as to hold themselves to consistent expectations. But the point is not whether you are consistent or inconsistent in your expectations, but whether you can get beyond being startled if you discover that you hold unrealistic expectations for life.

Bill's health crisis rudely awakened him to the unrealistic expectations he had for life and he felt betrayed. His awareness was the occasion of great suffering. As he struggled to make sense of his suffering, his expectations for life changed. And the occasion of Bill's suffering became the experience through which he resolved his conflict.

If I expect life to be unending,
*   then dying seems to be an illusion.*

When Bill's life was fairly secure and routine, it was easy for him to fall into assumptions that life, his at least, would continue uninterrupted. He saw tragedy striking others, but with care and determination, he thought he could preserve his own.

Bill believed staunchly that he would never die—not the "real Bill." When he began to receive visitors at the hospital, even though he knew his diagnosis, he kept assuring them that he would be "just fine in no time." When his physical appearance began to deteriorate, he would ask rhetorically, "Don't we believe in immortality?" For Bill, personal immortality was the basic tenet of his faith. He believed himself to be "naturally immortal."

When his friends from church came to visit, they spoke

about how he must maintain "Christian hope." By that they seemed to mean that if Bill would keep up his will, and his hopes high, he could overcome his disease and leave the hospital "good as new." Dying was an illusion to them, too.

Holding to this interpretation of life carries at least two risks. The first is that such a faith does not permit the person experiencing crisis to acknowledge basic change and real loss. When Bill's health began to deteriorate markedly, he began to question whether he had "real faith." His friends tried to encourage him with declarations that *if* he kept up his faith, he would be "good as new." By implication, this suggested to Bill that if he did not recover, it would be because his faith had not been strong enough. When Bill did not become "good as new," these friends ceased coming to see him.

The second risk to this interpretation is that it depends on an out-dated understanding of biology. In the days when we knew very little about the mind, it was assumed that the mind was a separable entity from the body because it was thought to be the "seat of the soul." In those days, there was no awareness of how our hormones and blood circulation can alter basic thought patterns as well as behavior patterns. "Train the mind properly," "believe correctly," "have the right kind of faith," and nothing that happened to the body could touch the mind. We now know that our minds, and the thoughts we have, are integral to and largely dependent on a relatively healthy body. As a matter of discipline for living a healthy and moral life, we do need to train our minds. But mind-training does not prevent our having to live with the consequences of bodily failure, or struggle with the suffering involved when our expectations do not conform to reality. Nor are we released from the guilt we feel when we are not able to "will away" our dying.

If I live life as a vocation,
   then dying is an intrusion.

Bill began to shift interpretation of his health crisis from dying as an illusion to dying as an intrusion. Had he not been living a good, moral life? Had he not been one of the best drivers on the road? When his buddies came from work to see him, they would reminisce about Bill's adventures and exploits: how he was the only one to drive through the worst storm of the year; how he had been shot at when defying a wild-cat strike; how he had never had a road accident. "What a great guy you are Bill! What a shame this is happening to you."

Bill did find some comfort in reflecting on the good he had done in his life. "Dying may be cutting off my life, but it can't take away from me what I've done." For Bill, this interpretation was but a transition. There are many of us, however, who use similar interpretations of life as our religion. "Life is defined by the good we do." Hope is based on the expectation that one can live long enough and well enough to complete one's purpose in living. The health of society depends on the great majority of us living life as a mission, and most of us get considerable satisfaction from our vocation, so long as we can see the good we do. But let the times change, let our vocation no longer be needed, let a new generation choose different styles of living, let us be forgotten, and we risk losing our sense of worth. Then the "real I" is not only intruded upon by dying but consumed by feelings of worthlessness.

If life is a threat,
   then dying is an escape.

Bill's disease became very painful. Medications could help relieve him for a time, but they also dulled his mind. Bill wanted to be able to converse with his family, so he resisted taking any more medication than he had to. As each breath became more and more painful, as he saw the suffering of his family, life became a threat. Bill found himself wondering if the joys and happiness of life had all been an illusion. He prayed to die, then he could escape both the pain of his disease and the suffering of his conflicts.

Interpretation of life as a threat was a new experience for Bill. He had always felt quite secure. Some people, however, know life only as oppression and insecurity. Few moments are free from wondering where the next threat to survival will come. Religion for them becomes a matter of survival through escape. For them, hope is based on the expectation that they will be able to reach a place or a status free from the forces that seem to be destroying them.

Whatever the reasons for this interpretation of life, whether social, family, or personal crisis, death as an escape carries a risk. While release from pain and terror may be desired, it may be so overwhelming a concern that other conflicts, such as those of love and loss, are ignored. This interpretation is so self-centered it does not permit release from interpersonal conflict between sufferer and those touched by his suffering. Like medication that only dulls the senses, death as an escape releases the sufferer from pain but not from the cause of the suffering. But then, sometimes, a person is given no other option.

If I accept life as a gift,
   then dying is part of the given.

Before the advent of hospital care, the dying patient had the opportunity to complete one final task—to teach his relatives and friends how to "die well." In the Middle Ages, preparation to die was called *ars moriendi*—the art of dying well.

Little books of devotions were written, not to picture the ravages of the plague, or to warn the reader of the consequences for failing to prepare for one's end, but to give "a complete and intelligible guide to the business of dying, a method to be learned while one is in good health and kept at one's fingers' ends for use in that all-important and inescapable hour." [1] Bill, while well, would have resisted looking at such a book. His conscious efforts had been directed to the belief that life was unending. Ironically, the fairly slow progress of his disease, with as much suffering as it caused, permitted Bill to work through his interpretation of living to the point that he could affirm life, yet accept his own dying.

When he tried to pretend that he did not really have a disease, that dying was an illusion, Bill had hoped for the miracle that would turn the clock back to the time when life was routine and he felt secure. To give the weight of sacred authority to his expectation, he proclaimed his wish as "Christian hope." But when he could not manage the pretense of health any longer, he based his hopes for worth on his vocation and the good works he had performed. After several months of illness, not only his good works, but he, himself, seemed to have been forgotten. His close friends seemed to have tired of coming to visit. Bill found no release in this interpretation. And his interpretation of dying as an escape spoke more to the pain of living than his sense of self-worth.

When Bill began to reflect on how precious, though fragile, life is, on how quickly security can become insecurity, on how basic change seems to characterize life, he learned to interpret his life in an entirely different way. Confessionally, gently, he spoke of how so much of what he treasured in life had come not as a reward because he deserved it or be-

cause he had earned it, but as a gift. Maybe dying was a part
of that gift. Maybe he had overlooked the real meaning of
his life. Rather than being obsessed with preserving himself.
he began to reach out to his family to share the suffering they
had in common. Ironically, as he adjusted to the realities of
his crisis, as he permitted himself to let go of old expectations,
as he touched and allowed himself to be touched with love,
he was released from his conflict. He still was in pain and he
continued to degenerate physically. But now he could affirm
life and face his dying.

This interpretation of life carries a profound risk with it,
too. It requires acknowledging loss, pain, suffering, frustrated desires, and uncompleted goals as a part of living.
Rather than affirming human perfectability, it acknowledges
personal frailty. But it is based on the premise that even
though men are mortal, mortal characteristics do not cut one
off from the purpose of life. To put this in theological language: neither loss, nor suffering, nor even dying, can cut us
off from the Giver of life.

The art of dying has not been lost, though for most of us
the scene and setting for its dramatic resolution have shifted
from the intimacy of the home to the public life of the hospital. What Bill discovered during his hospitalization was
that he could "die well." But not, as he put it, "until I
found out that it was the Serpent who sold me that bill of
goods about never dying."

Whether you have identified with any of Bill's interpretations of life is not important. What is important is for us
to understand that the meaning of "dying" is based on our
expectations for living. When crisis befalls us, we will discover that as our expectations for living change, so too will
the meaning of dying. "For where your treasure is, there will
your heart be also." [2]

Can We Allow Dying to Be Part of Life?

Whether we can allow dying to be part of our life has profound consequences both for us and for the patient. Bill's transition in understanding what dying meant for him is not unusual for critically and terminally ill patients whose health crisis gives them time to work through their interpretations of the experience. Many of the six hundred patients followed in my research experienced a similar release. But some patients never were released from the suffering of their conflicts. Some of them weren't given the time. Others were not permitted to be released because of demands and expectations imposed on them by well-meaning relatives, friends, or health care workers whose own feelings became primary.

While health crisis in a loved one is always a shock, if we cannot accept the realities of the health crisis or adapt as fast as the patient does, we tend to act defensively in an apparent effort to protect our own emotions. This is called the Abandonment Syndrome. Almost all patients express fear that their condition will make them so unacceptable to those around them that they will be abandoned. Numerous studies have confirmed their fears. When a patient comes to a health care center, he is faced with a double burden: wrestling with survival and struggling to learn new expectations of those on whom he must now rely for his needs. He needs the familiar presence of family and friends all the more.

The patient may feel abandoned as the result of any of these occasions.

1. *A brief and formal monologue:* A physician, for example, may pop in on the patient, ask a few rhetorical questions such as, "You're looking better today aren't you?" and leave, appearing too busy to listen to intimate fears. A clergy-

man may call on a parishioner, say a few words of good cheer, offer a formalized prayer, and leave without ever knowing what is really troubling the patient. Nurses may place dying patients in dark corners of a ward, stop at the bedside only long enough to check vital signs, or make only mandatory visits. Friends and relatives may breeze in, inform the patient how he ought to be feeling, promise to stop by the next day, and never return again.

2. *Treating the patient as though disease or accident has turned him into a non-person.* This kind of abandonment is evident whenever people begin to talk about the patient in front of him as though he isn't there anymore. Even unconscious patients may hear.

3. *Ignoring or rejecting the cues the patient tries to give us that he wants to talk about his interpretation of what is going on.* When he says, "I think I'm going to die soon," and we respond, "Nonsense, you're going to be around for years"; when he says, "I guess no one cares for me any more," and we respond, "You're not the only patient, you know," we have informed the patient that his are not important feelings.

4. *Literal abandonment,* especially with patients in nursing homes. Many well-meaning close friends and relatives say that they no longer visit a loved one in a hospital or nursing home because: "I want to remember him the way he was," or "He doesn't even remember my name," or "Everything that can be done is being taken care of by the nurses," or "Everyone has to die alone." Perhaps being with the patient is too threatening. But even senile patients need to be physically stroked, spoken to, given gestures of affection.

We may be so troubled by fears of our own death or be so shocked by the implications of our loved one's crisis, that we have to separate ourselves from them in some way.

Abandonment is the most effective short-term defense mechanism we have, but it doesn't help the patient.

Many suggestions have been made to correct the Abandonment Syndrome. One suggestion often made is, "Let the patient return home to die." For some patients this may be an appropriate suggestion, but not for all. We need to remember that close friends and relatives are as susceptible to the temptation to abandon the patient as hospital personnel. Some patients may receive competent care at home, but many may not. The recurring statement, "I'm so thankful to be here in the hospital; now maybe I can get some peace," is a grim reminder that a patient often finds himself in conflict with well-meaning relatives whose own needs do not accommodate themselves easily to the needs of the patient.

My suggestion to correct the Abandonment Syndrome is to remind friends, relatives, and health care personnel that the patient needs all of them. They tend to balance one another's talents and deficiencies. Hospital personnel have skills few relatives, even those trained as nurses or doctors, can provide. Part of their expertise is made possible by an emotional distance that allows them to accept a patient's needs for what they are. These needs may be too threatening to grieving friends and relatives. Yet, hospital personnel, try as they may, cannot give the kind of personal affection a patient has come to trust from family and friends. Each relative and friend is a unique individual. Each responds to the patient in a special way. Each brings a different emotional strength that may help the patient regain a sense of equilibrium.

All of us—relatives, friends, or health care personnel—tend to abandon the patient when something about his crisis or his needs threatens our own emotional stability. No one can pretend to be able to meet all of a patient's needs. Only as we recognize our own limitations and work together can we overcome the Abandonment Syndrome. And only as we work through those things that threaten us emotionally can we adequately respect our own health.

What does "dying" mean? When it is not a part of the phenomena of our life or that of a loved one, it may have no apparent meaning. When "dying" touches us or one of our loved ones, it may be so threatening that we have to deny that it is part of life. But whatever it means, it is based on the expectations we have of life. For some of us, dying means the experience of discovering who we really are. Then "dying" becomes the most revelatory event of our life.

2

When Dying Means Loss

Blessed are those who mourn, for they shall be comforted.

MATT. 5:4 RSV

"Dying" may be defined in many ways, but universal to all definitions is "loss"—separation from persons we love, from places or objects we treasure, from a part of our self-identity. We develop an understanding of dying from the ways we have learned to cope emotionally with the wounds of loss.

When we, or those close to us, are dying, we *feel* our loss. Some of us are very guarded about showing our emotions. We have not learned adequately what to do with our feelings. Those of us who have learned to be more open and honest with our feelings have the best prognosis for healing from our loss.

John was a muscular 48-year-old assembly line worker. The death of his mother was a devastating blow. Though John took great pride in his strength and to his friends appeared to be emotionally very strong, he was quite dependent on his mother and relied on her even after his marriage. He seemed to have exaggerated feelings of competition about his work and his play. He always "had to win." Consequently, he never permitted himself to appear as losing. Even though his mother had been dead six months he would not mention her name or allow others to do so in his presence. It seemed at first as though he felt no loss, but after a time he became sullen, depressed, and aloof.

Mike also worked on an assembly line. He lost his parents in an automobile accident when he was forty-two years old. Initial reaction to the death of his parents was shock, but then he cried freely, talked about his childhood experiences with his family, and participated in overt rituals of mourning with his wife and children. Mike had always been a warm, friendly person. But of more importance emotionally, he did not feel he always had to win. He could tell jokes on himself and he readily acknowledged mistakes.

Learning to Cope With Loss

We are born with the *ability* to adapt to change, but we all must *learn* how to cope with loss. And, in fact, if you are able to read this book, you have already learned some rituals for coping with your losses. But not all ways for coping are healthy ways. I think it is no accident that the reason I came to know John and Mike is that John was admitted to the hospital with cancer of the colon eleven months after his mother's death. I met Mike when he came to visit John. Clinical studies show that despite obvious differences in family composition, religion, ethnic origin, and socio-economic status, repressing our feelings over loss prevents us from adapting to the change our loss has brought to our lives and may lead to mental and physical breakdown.

What do we need to learn in order to cope with loss?

First, we need to learn to respect the natural psychological process that helps us recover emotionally from the shock of loss and from the suffering of deprivation. Our natural way is to mourn or grieve. To mourn is to ventilate feelings. This ventilation sets us to working through emotions and expectations associated with the person or object we are losing or the loved one we have lost. We also grieve over things we can no longer do. Mourning involves testing the reality of permanent absence, reassessing identification with the loved person, reexamining our expectations of the loved person, and transferring to and investing emotionally in new people.

Not all of us have learned to mourn effectively. How the following children were taught may make the point clear. Pat thought that each of her children should have a pet. "It builds responsibility," she said. She daily monitored the children's feeding, cleaning, and caring of the pets, but she never did their chores for them. One day she noticed that her daughter's goldfish was floating upside down. Quick scrutiny revealed that the fish was already dead. When her daughter came home, Pat allowed her to discover her loss. Together, they took the fish out of the bowl and put it in fresh water. Within reason, Pat cooperated with every other suggestion her daughter made for trying to revive the pet. Finally, the little girl broke down, crying, and said, "My fish is dead," and Pat could comfort her. Not until that point would the little girl tolerate being comforted. Pat helped her daughter make a cardboard coffin, and her husband helped bury the cherished pet in the back yard. No suggestion was made about replacing the fish until it came from the little girl. Until then Pat and her husband helped their daughter grieve over the lost goldfish. Pat used rituals of openness and acceptance to instruct her children. The day came when the little girl announced that she was ready for a new pet. She had been healed.

Agnes instructed her children differently—with rituals of denial and defensiveness. She objected to her son, Pete, having a dog. She doubted that he would take very good care of it. There were frequent lapses of responsibility when Agnes had to care for the pet; nevertheless, the dog seemed a healthy outlet for Pete's affections. One afternoon, the dog was hit by a car. Agnes was horrified. Frantically, she buried the remains in the back lawn and scrubbed the pavement so that the child would not see any stains when he returned from school. After checking with her husband, she dashed to the local pet store and had a new pet waiting for Pete when he came home. There was not much emotion expressed in their household, either joy or sorrow. Agnes answered Pete's questions honestly, though reluctantly. But she kept emphasizing that he had a new dog; he ought not mourn. When the boy did cry, his father made him stop.

Agnes, like many parents, did not want "to inflict suffering" on her children. "They will have to face up to that soon enough as it is." She tried to pretend that the new puppy would fill any place in Pete's emotions left empty by the death of *his* dog. While "it just seemed best" to Agnes, she robbed her son both of the opportunity to learn that loss can be faced openly and that his feelings were appropriate. Denial is our first reaction to loss. Agnes unwittingly tried to make it the lasting reaction. Rather than keeping her children from knowing about irreversible loss and suffering, she conveyed to them the notion that loss, and their emotions as a reaction to loss, are taboo.

Both mothers were well-meaning. Pat respected her daughter's feelings and as a result helped the girl learn to honor the natural way of healing. But because Agnes and her husband were uncomfortable with their own emotions, Pete's expression of grief was threatening to them. Their behavior taught Pete that he ought not trust his own feelings. Healing from his loss would be difficult.

If the first thing we need to learn in order to cope with loss is to respect our emotions of mourning, a second is to learn that mourning is a developmental and life-long process. We can expect to mourn only within the limits of our emotional capacity. When loss is encountered as a child, grieving is a feeling only. When loss is encountered as an adolescent, grieving is both a feeling and a concept. When loss is encountered as an adult, grieving is not only a feeling and a concept, but also evaluated behavior. Following is a brief description of how we develop our capacity for mourning.

The Child's Encounter with Loss

The way a child reacts to loss depends largely on his emotional age.[3] Children feel pain and they suffer emotionally, but they do not have an adult's logic by which to understand the experience. Consequently, their mourning is often abbreviated and left incomplete.

An infant who loses its mother through death or abandonment in the second or third month seems to experience distress when the "mother-figure" is changed, but distress can be relieved so long as the infant's needs are satisfied.[4] But loss experienced between six months and one year registers with more serious distress because the infant has become able to distinguish between *what* satisfies his needs and *who* does the satisfying. Should loss occur, the child does not automatically transfer emotional attachment for his mother to someone else.

Loss can be quite a shock to a young child because he has no innate notion that life ever ceases. But before the age of four years, he may begin to ask questions about dying, questions stimulated by the phenomena of autumn, death of a favorite pet, or the loss of a cherished person. His questions assume that there is a reason for everything. While he generally is not interested in the physiological aspects of death, he does want to know, "Where did grandma go?" "Why?" "How?" He may ask the same questions over and over again. Because he does not have a well-developed conceptual framework by which to interpret the answers, the child's questions seem new to him even though they are redundant to adults.

A child of five is able to see relationships, some causations, and some implications. But he is usually unable to put himself in another person's position; therefore he has great difficulty handling other people's mourning. One family received word of the death of a beloved grandmother. When his parents and two older sisters began to cry, Jimmie did too. But then he began to laugh. Indignantly, his sisters demanded that he explain his behavior. "Well, she will be back, won't she? Why be sad?"

We all have a limited capacity for grieving, but the child is even more limited. Often confused by the seemingly long rituals adults use for grieving, children are usually ready to return quickly to their routine rhythms of living. A child's capacity for dealing with loss is limited.

Denial is a child's initial reaction to loss. His rhythms of mourning are usually broken by periods of denial and "make believe," either that the crisis has never happened, or that he has the magical power to make the deceased come back alive. What impact denial has on his emotional development depends largely on how well people around him react to his behavior. A college student reports that when he returned home from school as a first-grader, he was told that his older sister had "gone away" and would never come back. Out of bewilderment, he asked questions only to have his parents respond with evasiveness. Finally they ordered him to stop asking anything more. Through the child's thought processes, which tend to be egocentric and concrete, he assumed that he must have done something wrong and that is why his sister went away. He suffered with his unmentionable guilt until he took a course about "death and dying" in college.

The young child evaluates events of loss in terms of what repercussions they have had on him. For the college student whose sister died when he was a first-grader, the repercussion was guilt. For another college student, it was anger. Sarah had been a "dying child." She reports that while she knew something was basically wrong, both from the way that she felt and the way people acted around her, her questions were rebuffed. An embarrassed nurse retorted that she was a "very naughty girl" for asking her questions about dying. In her bewilderment, infected by increasing anger, Sarah had the most distorted of fantasies. Sometimes she believed she was being eaten alive by frogs. At other times she pictured the doctors and nurses as wizards and witches who were changing her into an animal. Her mother and father appeared in her dreams as miniature toys, utterly helpless. Sarah alternated between roles of a little girl screaming for their help and of a heroine trying to rescue them. What was happening to her was incomprehensible. She had intense feelings but an inability to interpret the experience. Now as an adult, she works with critically ill children and tries "to help these children have a different ending to their nightmares."

Children use a great deal of fantasy in their efforts to grasp inexplicable phenomena. In the illustrations above, I have focused on children who have experienced loss first-hand. But children between the ages of five and puberty also work through notions concerning dying and loss in peer relationships. They speculate and create games. They play at "what it must be like." Anne Hebert Smith of New Haven tells about a group of black children in North Carolina. While waiting for their dance class to begin, they acted out their curiosity concerning dying by chanting:

> "Well, what's the news?"
>   "Well, *what is* the news?"
> "Auna Donna's dead!"
>   "Aunt Donna's dead?"
> "Well how did she die?"
>   "Well, *how* did she die?"
> "Well, she died like this."
>   "She died like this?"
> "Ugh! Ugh! Ugh!"
>   *(acted out with mock agony)*

If adults don't oppress his initiative, a child's questions concerning death arise out of his curiosity about how change through loss could have occurred. Some children express profound confusion in fantasy and bizarre games. Recent research suggests that all children have some confusion about inevitable and irreversible loss.

Because children have feelings but an incomplete capacity for interpreting the experience that stimulates these feelings, their healing process usually is incomplete until late adolescence or adulthood. But if the child is encouraged to share his emotions and how he perceives them, he learns that he is still acceptable and lovable despite his loss. He can continue to grow emotionally as well as physically.

The Adolescent's Encounter with Loss

The adolescent is able to understand the full implications of dying and the finality of death. He has the capacity for both feeling and interpreting experiences of loss. He has well-developed ways for testing reality and has capacities to adapt

to the change loss brings. Generally, however, his overt behavior is significantly different from the patterns of mourning among mature adults. Like children, the adolescent tends
to overcompensate for his feelings of grief by fantasizing
either return of the loved person or power to reverse the
loss. The intensity of this contradiction in behavior seems to
be in direct proportion to the adolescent's progress in estab-
lishing independence from his parents. The more insecure he
is in his own identity, the more he tries to over-compensate
for his inadequacies.

The normal adolescent, whether having developed a very
strong self-concept or a weak one within the family struc-
ture, must be able to identify those points that differentiate
him from his parents before he can become an autonomous
adult. In order to do this, he no longer is dependent on
adults as he was as a child. He turns to his peers for identity
support. It is from close peer competitors that a boy, for
example, can estimate his own prowess—whether his mind
is keen, his body is strong, his accomplishments worthy. It is
from her peers that a girl learns what is mature and what is
immature, even though the peer group's definitions may be
quite at odds with those of adults. Hair and clothing styles
often reflect the definitions of the peer group. At the very
same time, however, the adolescent seemingly needs his parents, or other authority figures, in order to have a mark by
which to measure his development into adulthood.

Research on the emotional needs of adolescents in times
of crisis suggests that the overwhelming majority fear loss of
those closest to them—both their friends and family. And
they fear isolation. Unfortunately, at the time an adolescent
needs support from his family he also seeks approval of his
own peers who often set themselves in opposition to an
adult's identity. Competition between peers and parents to
influence an adolescent produces conflict under very normal

circumstances. This conflict becomes intense in a crisis of loss. The adolescent's signals of needs may be confusing to adults, as, in fact, the adolescent's own feelings are confusing to himself. Both close fellowship and solitude are important for the adolescent in crisis. Every adolescent needs access to adults who are loving and tolerant of his erratic behavior.

In *Growing Up Absurd*, Paul Goodman argues that our society's great indulgence for children makes it difficult for even the most ambitious adolescent to prove himself with *real* work for real rewards. Those adolescents struggling with disease, who are not permitted by well-meaning adults to struggle with the reality of their disease in ways that seem "real" to them, are either forced back into a posture of infant dependency or into exaggerated rebellion for independence. For an adolescent patient, it is bad enough that he must wrestle with a body deteriorating at the same time that his own peers are filling out in full bloom of maturity, but it is intolerable to have one's sense of worth snatched away either by those the patient loves or with whom he competes.

While adolescents have the capacities for both feeling and conceptualizing experiences of loss, their judgments about the implications of their experiences are often quite immature and their healing may be left incomplete. Often an adolescent treats all loss with the same intensity. When Bob lost his favorite coat for example, he thought his life was ruined. Mary thought she could never recover when her boyfriend left her, but she was as emotionally distraught over losing her athletic pin. Unlike children, adolescents have the capacity to conceptualize experiences of loss. But unlike adults, they have not had the experience to evaluate their concepts of loss. One mark of maturity is the ability to differentiate degrees of loss.

The adolescent's encounter with loss is far less affected by whether adults respond with exactly the right words as by the "feeling tones" with which they respond. If adults convey to the adolescent that feelings of, or questions about, loss are inappropriate, the adolescent is thwarted in his mourning. Only as he is encouraged to express himself and to evaluate what his loss means to him, can he resolve the conflicts of his experience and thereby be free to move on to discover new concerns, curiosities, and loves of living.

The Adult's Encounter with Loss

By the time many of us reach adulthood, we have learned that our days are numbered, and we try to use our life wisely. To know that we are mortals does not keep us from feeling the excruciating sting of loss. Hopefully our knowledge does permit us to trust that even though we experience irreversible loss we are given the capacities to go on living. Mature mourning permits us to adapt to change forced by loss.

John Bowlby and C. Murray Parkes identify four phases of healthy mourning: 1) numbness, 2) yearning for the deceased person or lost object, 3) disorganization and despair, and 4) reorganization.[5]

Numbness is a characteristic of emotional shock and is exhibited both by outright denial that loss has taken place and by stupor. Some people may believe that they are functioning normally at time of loss, but objective observation indicates the contrary.

The second phase is characterized by painful yearning for the deceased person or lost object. The mind becomes obsessed with everything that can be recalled about the deceased. Familiar sounds and smells may, at least momentarily, make the mourner believe that their loved one has returned. Anger at being left alone, guilt over omissions in their relationship, and separation from familiar patterns of life shared with another—all these deepen the pain of separation.

The period of disorganization is marked by the struggles of survivors to compensate for the role no longer played by the deceased. In the family constellation, there are problems over who will assume vacated roles. For a surviving spouse, there not only is the need to compensate for former dependence on the deceased but the uncertainty over what degree of independence is either possible or desirable.

Reorganization usually occurs gradually. But some people seem to be relieved of their grief in a relatively short time. In some cultures, the period of reorganization is marked by a ritual, such as a feast on the anniversary of the death, which signals that the period of mourning is over. But what is important is when, in one's heart, the deceased is permitted to be released. Then healing takes place, and one's love may again be directed to others.

Adults who suffer loss of someone close to them sometimes mourn with behavior more appropriate to a child. Analysis usually uncovers unresolved loss from childhood or adolescence, evidence that for some reason the mourning process was left incomplete. Mark is an example.

Mark was thirty-five when his mother died. He appeared to have a stable home life and a satisfying career, but he began to exhibit erratic behavior soon after his mother's funeral. He failed to complete assignments at work, his sleep patterns were disturbed, and he seemed aloof from his family. When Mark came for counseling, he said he was coming to satisfy his family, that there was nothing wrong with him. Yet, even in the first session, he broke down in tears and began to speak of "Auntie." When asked why he called his mother "Auntie," he reacted with surprise. "I don't. That is what I called my aunt." Mark remembered his aunt as a surrogate mother. She had lived next door to his parents, had provided him with a great deal of companionship, and had taken care of him while his mother had been confined to bed with a long illness. Auntie died when Mark was twelve. The occasion of his mother's death stimulated repressed conflict. Mark, as a child, had not been able to understand his aunt's death and in his subconscious, at least, he had tried to keep her within grasp.

Mourning is our natural way of healing from loss. When our grieving process is healthy, we are able to express our feelings, conceptualize or make sense out of the experience, and we are able to come to a weighted assessment of what the experience means to us. Not every loss will be felt with the same intensity.

Our Encounter with Another's Loss

Even though we may have developed healthy ways for handling loss, we may fall into what I call the "Surrogate Suffering Syndrome" when we encounter another's loss. It is one thing to work through our own feelings of loss; it is quite another to realize that we must let others work through their sense of loss, too. Most of us try to shield our loved ones from suffering, particularly when the one we love is a child. But, as noted above, even children must be able to work through feelings of loss. The following examples demonstrate why.

Two six-year-old children had leukemia. Martha, mother of the first child, had great difficulty handling her own emotions. She was often hysterical, anxious, and guilt-ridden. She conveyed to both her friends and the hospital personnel that no one should permit her child to suffer. "Don't explain anything to him. Don't play with him. Leave him to me." Her child in turn, reflected the emotions and behavior of his mother, largely it seemed because those were the emotions she would accept from him. Each step of therapy was a hassle. Panic seemed to infect the child every time someone came into his room. He was confused and frightened.

Geri, mother of the second child, maintained a sense of composure, courage, and competence even though there were times when she freely cried. She identified times and circumstances when she needed help from others, particularly from her husband, and assumed a healthy dependence on the hospital staff. Her son exhibited similar behavior. Even as he was dying, he insisted that he do some things for himself. Despite the usual side-effects of his disease and therapy, which sometimes lead to disorientation and depression, the patient seemed to have a sense of confidence that he would be taken care of.

For both children, the disease was debilitating. For the first child, there was additional suffering with fears of being unable to cope.

The attempt to shoulder a patient's suffering for him is as futile as it is to try to do his dying for him. The attempt seems to be motivated by a mixture of good will and guilt, love and hostility, service and need to control. Every attempt to be the surrogate sufferer imposes an additional burden of loss on the patient.

Attempts to be another's surrogate sufferer or attempts to stifle our own feelings are not healthy ways to handle loss. Mourning is our natural way for coping with loss. When our grieving process is healthy, we are able to express our feelings, conceptualize or make sense out of the experience, and we are able to come to a weighted assessment of what the experience means to us. "Blessed are those who mourn, for they shall be comforted."

3

When Dying Means Change

For every matter has its time and way, although man's trouble lies heavy upon him.

ECCLES. 8:6 RSV

Dying means change. Even when we think we are prepared, as the time approaches, most of us fear that we will not be able to cope. But "every matter has its time and way." We not only change but we can adapt to the realities of most crises no matter how offensive or radical.

But change may not be our true fear. Many patients and relatives initially did say that they feared they could not change. On further reflection they discovered they were far more threatened by the possibilities that they would lose their humanness or their dignity in the process of change.

"Dignity" ought not be confused with "pride." Pride implies an exaggerated sense of self-worth and is the opposite of "humility." Both a proud and a humble person have a sense of dignity. Dignity stands for the self-assessment we have of ourselves as persons. It is the sense of worth that comes with having the freedom and responsibility to make judgments about what is proper and improper. "Self-reli-ance"—the ability to make decisions for oneself—was the word most frequently used by patients to describe what dig-nity meant to them. It may have been the decision whether to submit to surgery or to chemotherapy. It may have been making the simple choice of whether they would eat jello or cottage cheese for lunch. But it was *their* decision. We ac-knowledge another's dignity when we honor his sense of propriety and his right to make decisions about himself.

We are changed by dying. The process of change, whether for the patient or for us, follows a fairly common pattern of behavior.[6] We feel shocked, then we need to ventilate our feel-ings of anguish. Given time, we are then able to reassess who we are as a result of the change forced on us. Perhaps we can better relate to others, and be addressed by them, with dignity if we understand the psychodynamics of change.

When We Are in Shock

Shock is the first psychodynamic in adapting to change forced on us by health crises and usually takes one of two forms: denial or panic. Denial is what has been called the human shock-absorber to tragedy. It is the way our emo-tions are temporarily desensitized and our sense of time tem-porarily suspended in our attempt to delay the consequences of the crisis. This permits us to "have time" to marshall our inner resources and to search for an appropriate response to an otherwise overwhelming threat.

Judy's behavior is an example of the use of denial. Judy was a beautiful young woman. Up until the time of her automobile accident she had been vivacious and healthy. Now her injuries left her paralyzed from the waist down. Any parent knows the infant's immense sense of achievement when he can sit up, crawl, and then walk; imagine what her loss of mobility meant to Judy. It was devastating. Psychologically, it took Judy much longer than it took her friends and relatives to adapt to the realities of her accident. She would greet visitors with the demand, "Nothing is wrong, so don't be upset!" Not unlike dazed accident victims in the emergency room who rise up off a stretcher in spite of broken bones and injured organs, Judy could not function realistically.

The appearance of shock and the use of denial may be quite inconsistent. To one person, such as the physician or the spouse, the patient will show massive denial: "I'm all right!" Yet, to another person, such as a sympathetic friend, nurse, or chaplain, the patient will be quite open with his feelings. It may not seem appropriate to share some realizations with some people; with others the patient may share deepest feelings. Why? The patient may feel safer by holding people with professional responsibilities at a distance. Or the patient may be able to sense that those closest to him are in shock themselves. Perhaps the patient's sense of propriety has been violated. The health care staff may have been curt toward the patient. Perhaps the patient's sense of modesty was violated. Sometimes unwitting but hurtful things were said. These, and similar situations, make the patient feel that he has lost a part of his dignity, and he is shocked.

Denial sometimes takes the form of displaced concern. The patient may be in critical condition, yet deny any concern for himself while expressing great concern about another patient. Sometimes denial takes the form of what is meant to be objective observation. This form of denial is frequently used by relatives. They may be deeply shocked about the loved one's health crisis, yet they try to act as though they are emotionally detached. All of these forms of denial lack the spontaneity that would be an expression of true feelings—anger, terror, offendedness. In denial, feelings are temporarily frozen.

Panic is the opposite of denial. When all structures of stability in our life seem to have been destroyed, our emotions have no limit of expression. Hysteria, psychosis, or irrational suicide are forms of panic. But whatever the form, to the person in panic, "the world has come apart." Intense anxiety, exaggerated excitement, paranoidal ideas may occur for a short duration. Providing no physical harm results, such manifestations of panic can be brought under control by someone exercising calm and authoritative leadership. Of longer duration, these manifestations of panic may need the assistance of a psychiatrist. Frequently a person in panic will grind through all of his emotional gears in a desperate attempt to find one that will work to restore a sense of order. "Where can I turn, where can I turn?" was the one coherent phrase used by a woman whose denial had been stripped away. Her world had become "topsy-turvy."

Several general principles may guide relatives, friends, and health care staff in helping a person in shock:

1. We need to be as calm as we can and avoid inconsistency and judgmentalism. If we ourselves are in shock, especially if bordering on panic, we need to let someone who can be more detached offer primary care. There is nothing more contagious than panic, nor more reassuring than calmness, to a person in shock.

2. We need to use calm but direct and specific language, speaking to him by name and with direct eye contact.

3. We may need to assist him to identify reality factors, such as time, place, and the name of people around him, to help him reorient himself.

4. We should, as much as possible, avoid trying to force the person in shock to make decisions.

5. We must respect his use of denial mechanisms as he copes with his crisis. We all use denial from time to time as a defense mechanism in our attempts to restore order to the chaos of a crisis. It is far more healthy emotionally for our loved one to use denial than to be panic-stricken.

How We Are Released from Shock

Neither denial nor panic can long be sustained emotionally. The question, "What has happened?" soon gets translated into a question of anguish, "Why has this happened to me?"

We are released from shock either by the ventilating or withholding of emotions. Freud observed accurately that whatever experiences we have are incorporated into our unconscious and will be expressed overtly in some form of behavior. Or to put it another way—whatever emotionally goes down has to come up. We can't dispose of emotional upset simply by ignoring it and pretending nothing has happened.

When denial has been used, even with partial success, to muster enough courage to face change, the patient can begin to externalize his emotions. It may take some form of emotion such as grief or anger. But whatever the form, it is a catharsis. To be able to cry, for example, is to recognize that our emotional system, like our bloodstream, has to be purified. As one patient put it, "When I cry, I am emptying my emotional bladder and it brings as real a relief as elimination." It is not always easy for health care workers, friends, and family to distinguish between a patient's catharsis and panic. But unlike the cries of panic which indicate that the patient fears he is out of control, catharsis is used to recover one's composure, and it is easily distinguishable by its consequent release.

Unfortunately we may be so unnerved by a patient's catharsis that we project our own feelings of near panic onto his behavior. Sometimes visitors become very uncomfortable when they find their loved one crying, and they will either try to make him stop themselves or call one of the staff to make him stop. In such a case I ask the persons who called if they think they would cry under similar circumstances. Almost always they answer, "yes." But still, they may be unnerved by seeing "my patient" or "my friend" catharting emotionally. How emotion is expressed is largely determined by what the culture permits. But emotion will be expressed in some way as the person in shock adapts to change.

When emotion is not expressed openly, either because of the individual's internal controls or because of society's expectations, anger is turned upon one's self as guilt, and release from shock is expressed as depression. It is as though the patient sees his crisis as punishment justly applied. I use the word "depression" as a description of the sense of particularized loss of worth: "I deserve what has happened to me." I am well aware of the word's strict usage in psychiatry, but as used there, it is impossible to make the needed distinction with "despair," which will be mentioned later.

When Mrs. A., a woman in her fifties, was diagnosed with Hodgkins Disease, she struggled with real courage to make sense of her situation. She was particularly susceptible to crying following chemotherapy. She would think about the very active life she had led, a life filled with service to others, and think of all that was left to do. She would think of her family, who, even though strong and independent in their own ways, were in other ways very dependent on her. "You know, I realize how much people have depended on me when I see how those things that I used to do simply don't get done any more. I don't want to die. I am still very much needed here." When she was quiet, she was depressed, and her friends and family taxed their abilities in trying to elevate her mood. They behaved as though somehow her depression was a figment of imagination or breakdown of her mind. They kept telling her, "Your disease is arrested. You're okay now. Your worries are all in your head." This, despite the fact that her physical condition had been greatly altered by the disease, that she had to go through all of the complications of her therapy every six weeks, and that she no longer had the energy to do any more than to move from bed to chair. When she tried to talk about those things that were most important to her, she would sometimes cry, only to be told by them, "Stop it! Don't you dare cry!" She was caught in a double bind. She was neither supposed to be depressed nor was she permitted to cathart. She was thwarted in her feelings as she attempted to be released from the conflict generated by her question, "Why me?"

Both relatives and health care personnel need to learn how to respect depression. As one patient suffering from cervical cancer put it, "How inappropriate it is for the physician to come in and tell me 'Depression is not allowed on my ward,' as though somehow or another I do not have a right to grieve over the loss that I am feeling. When I feel blue, I have a right to feel blue. It is appropriate to feel blue." Only as patients are permitted to grieve can they be expected to have the confidence to face change. Many patients long ago discovered how they can best externalize deep emotional conflict. It is important for us all to give both opportunity and assurance to the patient that emotions can be externalized in ways he feels are appropriate and relieving.

A patient's anger because of illness or accident is neither unusual nor inappropriate. It is the recognition that he has sustained real loss. Patients will wrangle, "Why me?" or,

"Why did I let this happen?" Most patients gain release from shock in both catharsis and depression. Rather than being abnormal, a patient's short-term depression is appropriate. If a patient did not become depressed at times, it would be uncharacteristic behavior. But, hopefully, the patient can be assisted to externalize his anger so that the periods of depression become shorter and less severe. To ask, "Why me?" is the second step we take naturally when we are forced to change by health crisis. But for the patient to keep his sense of dignity, he must work "out," not keep "in," his feelings of anger, guilt, and disillusionment.

The same emotional dynamics apply to those of us who must adjust to health crisis of a loved one. If your family has not openly shared both joy and sorrow, you may fear that externalizing your true feelings will either be rejected as inappropriate by your friends and the health care staff or add an unnecessary burden to the patient. You, too, should ventilate your feelings, sometimes even publicly, so that your periods of depression can become shorter and less severe.

How We Try to Make Sense of Unwanted Change

We try to make sense of unwanted change by worrying about ourselves, by reassessing who and where we are in our world. We may not be as systematic in our measurements as was Benjamin Franklin who reported that he went through a check list every night to catch his errors. But we do reassess who we are when we realize "things have changed."

For a patient, assessment represents the attempt to answer the questions, "What has happened to me?" "What does this all mean?" "What's left of me?" Assessment is the attempt to readjust one's identity as a result of new and altering experiences. Crisis and illness alter the context for living.

"Who am I now?" If the patient perceives himself radically altered, with relationships ruptured, is it possible to be reconciled? If he has perceived himself as guilty of some wrongdoing, is it possible for him to understand being forgiven? If he has been acting out fears of being abandoned, is it possible to be reunited? These are the kinds of concerns with which the patient wrestles as he tries to assess *where* he is in an apparent attempt to rediscover *who* he is.

Assessing oneself raises many questions, and most patients need encouragement to ask them. It is not too difficult to distinguish between questions that seek data and questions which attempt to assess self-worth. Questions that seek data will be focused: "Why can't I get up?" "Why didn't you get here earlier?" "When is my next dose of medication?" These questions should be answered, if possible. Questions which attempt to assess self-worth tend to be more remote: "What do you think has happened to me?" "Do you think I'm feeling any better?" "Do you think I'm going to last very long?" Behind these spoken questions are hidden suspicions: "Will they listen to my *real* fears?" A patient tests our reactions to his questions. If we are to encourage him to articulate his suspicions about self-worth, we need to refrain from rendering opinions as an immediate response. We can assure him of the appropriateness of asking his questions and discussing his suspicions by responding acceptingly with a question in turn: "How does it seem to you?" The patient may then share his true feelings.

Hope, which centers on fulfilling expectations, may focus on getting well, but more often focuses on what yet can be done. It is expressed as having the chance to "finish my business," which may refer to putting financial affairs in order, or, as in lengthy illness, a desire for a quick end. In some illnesses, patients have only one hope: "All I want is to control this pain." Sometimes hope is based on a possible miracle that will reverse the degenerating character of illness. But most often, a patient hopes that he will be able to maintain his sense of dignity no matter what. Hope is a perspective and an assessment of what one can expect for himself. Staff and relatives may mistakenly hear this expression of hope as "denial" rather than accommodation to reality.

When we hear a patient say, "I just don't seem to love life anymore," this patient is depressed. But when we hear him say, "All life is tragic, why do we endure it!" it is a sign of despair. Symptoms of despair appear when depression is sustained and the factors which have depressed the patient have become diffuse and generalized. No longer is it just the self that seems to be out-of-joint, but all of life. Despair is the abandonment of hope. It is succumbing to the assessment that there is no more purpose to living. Unlike hope, which seems to be based on the patient's expectation that he can locate himself, despair seems to be based on his inability to find a perspective and he has the sense of being cut off, of being alienated.

Mrs. K. expressed both hope and despair during her terminal illness. At first, it seemed that no matter what was being done for her, she was anxious, not in a hostile sort of way, but always very tense. When I talked with her, she would look past my shoulder. I asked her one day, "Mrs. K., what is it that you keep looking for?"

"Well, I don't know."

"But you keep looking?"

"Yes."

"There's some reason; can you tell me what it is?"

"I don't know. It's just that nothing seems to make sense anymore."

"Are you hunting for a friend?" I asked.

"No."

"A relative?"

"I don't have any."

"Are you hunting for your physician?"

"I don't know. I think he was here already."

Checking with her physician, I found that he had had the same experience. When he came to see her, or when the nurses came to give her a bath or to distribute her medications, she was always looking past them as though waiting for something to happen or someone to come. The same thing occurred when her friends came to visit. But she could never put her finger on what she was looking for. It was to be cut off from she knew not what. The more the patient distanced herself, the more her friends and staff tended to regard her as an object, thereby reinforcing her loss of self-worth. They would talk about her to each other in front of her as though she weren't present. Her despair became their alienation.

One day the patient's demeanor changed. She no longer seemed to be overly-anxious. I asked her, "What is it that has changed for you?"

I was surprised at her answer. She said, "Now I know how I'm going to die. I don't have to worry anymore."

Note: She did not say, "Now I know that I'm *not* going to die; I don't have to worry about dying." That was not her concern. She was anxious to know how she was going to die so she could prepare for it. Now she knew. She had accepted her state of terminal cancer. She wasn't anxious about being caught off guard. The health care staff could tell her about what she could expect. She instructed her friends how to go about helping her put affairs in order. Adaptation for Mrs. K. did not come easily, but her despair was broken and her anxiety relieved. That didn't mean that she was well but it did mean, "I can cope with life. I can handle my disease. I can make sense out of it. I'm worth the effort."

Assessment represents the kind of tensions that have to be resolved when crisis has passed the first wave of intensity and we have time to reflect on who we are. We can do several things to assist a patient's struggles for self-assessment:

1. We can help him sort through his thoughts, in his own time and way, to help him determine just what resources and strengths he has left. But no patient can make a very realistic assessment if the significant people around him resist answering his requests for data. The excuse, "We haven't told him anything about his condition; we don't want to take his hope away from him," both erroneously supposes that the patient is asking for all there is that can be said about his situation and that the only ground for hope is to be cured. To the contrary, most patients will limit their questions to the amount of information they are prepared to handle, and many patients, after working through initial disappointment, will find hope even in the willingness of friends, relatives, and health care workers to treat them as functioning, competent adults.

2. When the patient exhibits symptoms of despair, it is often therapeutic to encourage him to be as specific as possible about his feelings. Focused, he can grasp and confront his crisis. Generalized and diffused, he cannot make a very orderly assessment about himself because his life seems chaotic. When a patient is in despair, he should have the assistance of someone trained in pychotherapy—a clinically trained chaplain, social worker, clinical psychologist, psychiatric nurse, or psychiatrist.

Things to Avoid As We Change

Being in shock, finding release through ventilation of emotions, and reassessing one's sense of worth represent the ways a patient adapts to change. We adapt to change the same way. And we, too, must respect our sense of dignity or we may be unable to provide the patient with the comfort and support he seeks. Because our rate of adaptation may not be the same as the patient's, or because we may need to "deny" that the patient's health crisis has forced basic change upon us, we may begin to feel that there is nothing we can do. Either we are still in shock or we think the health care personnel can provide all of the patient's needs. If we are not careful, we succumb to the Waiting Vulture Syndrome which occurs either when we refuse to respect our own emotions or when our mourning in anticipation of loss precedes the death of the patient.

Inez and her family were typical of this syndrome. Inez was a 43-year-old mother of two who was readmitted to the hospital with advanced cancer of the colon. Exploratory surgery found that her colon was totally blocked and that her cancer was spreading rapidly and widely. The patient, like her family, had come into the hospital fully expecting that her disease could be corrected by some medical procedure. Two previous admissions, with surgery, had relieved her cancer symptoms.

When Inez was told that she was inoperable, she responded to the physician with the rhetorical question, "Then that means that this will be my last hospitalization, won't it?" The physician was direct but not blunt in confirming her suspicion. The patient went into shock for a brief period of time, but after a similarly brief period of catharsis, set herself to the immediate task of getting her affairs in order.

The patient was quiet, articulate, and fully in command of her senses. At no time from the point of admission until she died was she without the presence of at least one member of her family. To the casual observer, to most of the staff, and to many of her relatives, she had a very strong ego. She played a strong role in family affairs. With her husband, however, she had a dependent personality which had endured his alcoholism and promiscuity with countless rhythms of martyred feelings, forgiveness, and reconciliation.

Her husband fled from the hospital upon receiving the physician's diagnosis and was found the following day in a tavern. Her children went into deep shock and had difficulty functioning anytime during the hospitalization. Several of the in-laws assisted Inez by running errands, collecting legal papers, and making telephone calls for her.

On the second day, most of the family spent their time crying or ventilating emotions in other ways. They would not grieve in front of the patient but did take turns being in the patient's room when they were in command of their emotions. The male members of the family had begun to concern themselves with three questions: 1) "Are we doing all that can be done to help her suffering?" 2) "How much more time is there?" and 3) "Is it all right to begin making 'final arrangements'?" To the first question, several of the hospital's staff gave sympathetic encouragement by suggesting ways the family could help. To the second question, the physicians and staff were noncommittal as to the precise time that death could be expected, but noted the patient's physical condition continued to deteriorate rapidly. To the third question, the staff encouraged them to "make arrangements" as rapidly as they felt competent.

On the third day after diagnosis, the patient had a siege of vomiting so violent the staff expected her to expire at any time. The patient's mind remained oriented, but focused on the single concern of how to be comfortable. Between bouts of nausea, Inez would concern herself with healing ruptures in family affairs and would call estranged members of the family together at bedside. By the end of the fourth day, the patient seemed ready to die and informed me, "I think all of my business is finished now." The family had, by and large, expressed their grief less frequently and for shorter periods of time. They had completed legal, financial, and funeral arrangements.

On the fifth day, the patient revived dramatically. She had ceased vomiting and was mentally so alert that she reported on the emotional and physical conditions of all her family with the same kind of detail she shared about herself. She was so bright in spirits that she was telling all who would listen, "I think I'll be going home again."

The relatives were physically and emotionally drained. They stood in the hallway and in the patient's room manifesting the physical characteristics of waiting vultures: drooped heads, shoulders falling forward, listlessness. Emotionally they seemed despondent and resigned. "There's nothing more we can do." They became increasingly angry; first with the patient, then with the staff, and finally with themselves. They expressed their hostilities toward the patient by avoiding eye contact with her, by not responding verbally to her comments and questions, and by long absences from her room. As one of her brothers blurted out, "If she's going to die, why doesn't she go ahead and die?" Then he quickly controlled himself and said, "I don't really mean that. I want her to live, but not if she's going to be eaten up with cancer some more." The family also expressed feelings about how the staff had "misled" them into thinking Inez was going to die. The staff had encouraged them to make "final arrangements." Now what would people think of them! What would Inez think of them if she were ever to find out? What were they to think of themselves? They felt guilty and angry for precipitously acting out their sense of loss when they were told that the patient was dying.

Many of the staff were very uncomfortable with the turn of events. They had expected the patient to continue going through the "stages all terminally ill patients are supposed to move," as a nurse put it. "Now she's out of sync!" They were embarrassed by the patient's failure to conform to preconceived ideas of terminal illness and by the relatives' hostility. "We've thought we were really doing everything so well."

By the end of the day, the patient felt very estranged, and said so. "It's as though I've become some sort of pariah. I'm being rejected because I'm not dying! Am I no longer a human being?" The relatives seemed unable to respond: "What more can we do, we've done everything we know how to do!" Thinking they could best support the relatives by agreeing, the staff assured them they *had* done everything they could. But they had not done everything.

One of the goals of therapy is to help patients, relatives, and health care personnel learn how to adapt to the reality of dying and to utilize their resources of grieving in order to cope with loss. Appearance of the Waiting Vulture Syndrome is a sign of both success and failure of therapy. It is the sign of success because it indicates that those afflicted have begun to process and express their sense of loss. It is a sign of failure, however, because it exposes those afflicted to the sense that they have precipitously accommodated themselves to a loss, and therefore leads one to assume that "there is no more relationship possible with my loved one" before death occurs. Feelings of helplessness ("There's nothing more we can do") are coupled with feelings of guilt ("We're ready too soon").

The error of the hospital staff was not their encouragement of the family to make "final arrangements" but their reenforcing the feelings of the family that "we've done everything we can." Even for a patient who is unconscious, it is important that relatives continue to show affection and assurance that they won't abandon him. Holding the patient's hand, brushing his hair, and massaging his arms and legs are ways of maintaining contact. This also applies to patients who seemingly no longer recognize friends and relatives. The Waiting Vulture Syndrome disappeared as soon as her family began to show Inez affection.

When Inez died on the eighth day after diagnosis, she died with a sense of ease. Several times during her final hour, she thanked those around her for their presence. She remained conscious until about fifteen minutes before her death. The relatives and staff seemed genuine in their self-assessment after her death: "We *did* do everything we could."

Dying means change. Whether patient or relative, we begin to change when we are shocked by the health crisis. If we try to pretend we aren't changed, we become alienated in our pretense. But if we can ventilate our emotions of anger, guilt, and bewilderment, we can begin realistic self-assessment which permits us to maintain our sense of dignity although our trouble lies heavy upon us.

4

When
Dying
Means
Conflict

Knowledge puffs up, but love builds up.

1 COR. 8:1 RSV

Interpersonal conflict can be more up-
setting than grief, fears of death, or
pain of disease, particularly for those of us who try to avoid
combative relationships. Few of us would will to do anything other than "the right thing" for a patient, yet clash
of opinion, competition with other "helpers," and differences of perspective can easily become occasions for emotional
battles. All of us who are acquainted with the patient
assume that we *know* the patient's needs. But our "knowledge" is not always in keeping with the patient's perspective
or based on the facts of the patient's crisis.

The bizarre struggle over interpretation of Carl's needs
is unusual only in the length of time it took for death to end
the matter. Carl, a tall, slender, five-year-old was admitted
unconscious to a hospital emergency room on a hot summer
day. He had been hit on the forehead in a teeter-totter accident at a nearby nursery school. His vital signs were unstable

and his eyes had markedly dilated. There were strong indications of brain stem involvement which would endanger proper functioning of his major organs.

Throughout the 15 days of Carl's hospitalization, his mother was cold, demanding, and overly anxious. Her demeanor fluctuated between expressions of guilt and feelings of anger. Little or no affection was expressed about the boy. Yet, when told that the patient's condition was hopeless, she would assert: "He'll be all right!" And she made this a demand on the physician.

Despite the advice of two neurosurgical consultants, the physician put the boy on a respirator and administered medication for sustaining vital signs. The physician frequently exploded at the nursing staff, warning them that if the boy died, "I will be sued, and you will be too!" He repeatedly changed orders and demanded excessive testing. He seemed, to everyone concerned, to be equally anxious about legal repercussions and his own fears of dying. "I cannot fail to keep this boy alive. I cannot let death win," became his obsession.

The nurses found the case particularly troubling. They were left to care for the child and to try to arbitrate between the child's needs and the needs of the mother and of the physician. Most of the nursing staff were either mothers or sisters of boys close to the age of the patient. They felt that he was being deprived and cheated out of one of the most valuable gifts of life—parental love.

After 15 days of "heroic efforts," the patient's heart failed and could not be revived. Autopsy confirmed what the neurosurgeons, nurses, and observers suspected 14 days previous: the boy's brain died soon after hospitalization. Through the use of "heroic efforts," certain vital signs were sustained for an extended period. But even life-preserving equipment cannot keep some tissues vital. The nursing staff had had to work with an increasingly stinking corpse. But for whose benefit? "Each of us felt that the care plan was being cruel to Carl," the head nurse reported. "We felt he should have the right to die in peace. He had been deprived of so much in life, why should he be deprived of his right to die?" Only the nurses, in this instance, had remained the patient's advocate. The mother's feelings of guilt, the physician's emotional confusion, and the hospital administrators' indifference were all justified by, "*I* know," but based on something other than the patient's needs.

I am sometimes asked by relatives, "If everyone wants to do the right thing for the patient, how can there be conflict?" It is a troubling question. Some people try to answer it in sweeping anger at hospitals and health care staffs: "Everyone should be allowed to die at home," as if the home setting is free of conflict for a patient. Others have argued that conflict arises as a result of ignorant behavior: "Only professional staff know how to care adequately for a patient," as though training makes the professional person the only expert about a given patient's emotional needs.

My own answer is based on my understanding of anxiety. When we are anxious about a patient's health crisis—and even experts are when a patient is critically or terminally ill —we become all the more concerned about our own behavior. The more anxious we become, the more we tend to attempt hiding our anxieties by being "knowledgeable" about the patient. We try to hide fears that "we may not be doing the right thing" or "we may not be doing all we can." I have been called as a consultant on a number of occasions when competition and conflict were so intense it never occurred to the combatants to consult the conscious patient about his needs.

In our own anxiety about other people's health crises, we tend to make their needs our own and we then try to meet the patient's needs in ways that we have learned may resolve our own emotional crises. But our ways often are not the ways of others who would seek to help the patient and, more importantly, not the ways of the patient. The following six examples are intended to show how differently people try to resolve emotional crises; such differences are the basis for much of the conflict which occurs in health crisis.

Herbert and Fern

Herbert and Fern lived all of their lives in the rural Midwest. They had no living children. Now that they were in their late fifties, they had drawn more and more into themselves emotionally and had only the smallest circle of friends. While bathing one evening, Fern noticed a lump in her breast and suspected that it might be malignant. Her mother and several other relatives had died of cancer. Fern shared her discovery with Herbert, but any motivation she might have had to see a physician was squelched by his response: "If you're going to have cancer, there's nothing we can do about it!" She did not visit a physician until the pain of an open lesion forced her to seek relief.

When the physician told the couple that there was nothing that could be done surgically, the couple showed no emotional reaction. They acted as though their suspicions were confirmed: "If you're going to have cancer there's nothing you can do about it." They had risked conflict at all costs, using what appeared to be passive strength to fight for control. They returned home and continued resolutely to carry on their lives' rituals without deviation. They displayed no emotions of enthusiasm or anguish. They preferred to trade away medical care for uninvolvement, honesty for quietness, and love for a truce. But their stoicism could not tame pain.

And the more Fern needed Herb's affection to counterbalance her suffering, the more he withdrew from her. Her dying meant the worst of tragedies to him, and his only defense was withdrawal. He expected his crisis to be avoided by emotional stoicism. The conflict they both had tried to avoid was now inevitable.

Rebecca

Rebecca was a patient in an intensive care unit. She had received severe burns in a home accident. Over 60 years of age, she was the mother of five children, and was very devout in her religious faith. Despite the fact that immense pain occurs with her kind of accident, she remained calm, undemanding, and pleasant. Even though the nurses kept saying to each other, "She must need pain medication," they never asked her. They were too much in awe of her serenity. Only after death did they learn from the family of her immense suffering.

Rebecca had seen her situation as part of life's mixture of temptation and righteousness. She thought of her behavior as being judged. She had been preparing for such crises most of her life. In the fight between good and evil, she was prepared to assume full responsibility for maintaining "a good battle." When asked by the family if she was in pain, she had exclaimed, "Oh yes, this is a *real* test of my faith, but I'll win." The family understood the context for such a witness of faith. To them, dying was the final and ultimate test of their religious beliefs. Consequently, they did not interfere on her behalf to ask for additional pain medication. That would have been a sign of weakness. They expected to overcome crisis by tenacious faith and serenity.

Unfortunately, a patient with this kind of personality trait seems to be the most neglected patient in health-care centers because his emotions are either misdiagnosed or misunderstood. Frequently, those who cannot believe that there can be a genuinely serene personality will define him as "stoical," "overly-dependent," or "maintaining mass denial." In either their hostility towards religion or their misunderstanding of the power of religious faith, staff may interpret behavior like Rebecca's as bizarre, peculiar, inappropriate, and even impossible.

Doctor John

Doctor John is a well-respected physician in his community. He exhibits all of those characteristics that give the impression of self-control, competence, efficiency, thoroughness, and principled behavior. But Dr. John can't handle emotional problems, particularly those surrounding a dying patient. He looks on dying patients as living proof of his failure as a physician.

Like other people who, in times of crisis, emphasize law over grace, principles over accommodation, and justice over forgiveness, Dr. John becomes very moralistic with patients who are critically and terminally ill. He makes it sound, when he talks at all, as though the patient has his crisis coming to him simply because he is in crisis. Dying is seemingly a moral judgment. It calls into question not only the righteousness of the patient, but the competence of the physician.

Belief in human perfectability, and "the-life-of-the-mind" tend to drive one toward mastery of thought processes and dominion of thoughts over feelings in order to guarantee preconceived avoidance. In times of crisis, spontaneity is thwarted and rhythms of living are transformed into inflexible rituals of orderliness. Several theories try to explain this behavior trait, but it is widely assumed that these people have the feeling that "I am loved not because of myself, but because of my behavior. I have to be perfect if I am to be loved."

Persons like Dr. John are found in disproportionate numbers among the health care professions. One of the reasons for entering these professions seems to be the need to overcome feelings of inadequacy, especially in the face of dying. And because they are efficient in order to check their fears, such health care workers expect patients to handle their anxieties in the same way. The more a patient became chaotic or ambiguous, the more obsessed Dr. John became with orderliness and efficiency.

Mabel

Mabel, a 50-year-old woman, had lived her whole life in a midwestern rural community. Her only interests were those of her family. Between caring for her home in early mornings and late evenings, she did heavy chores. She had no interests or hobbies which were distinctly her own. Always, she worked for her family. Mabel's husband and children would discuss politics at the table, but she seldom if ever rendered an opinion, and only then, after she was sure of her husband's stance. When she was diagnosed with cancer of the cervix, she was not informed of the diagnosis on orders from her family. Even after the disease had spread widely and she had been hospitalized, her family regularly lectured the staff about the necessity of keeping her diagnosis a secret.

The husband and children first channeled their energies into making up games to play with the patient. Then they established schedules for her in the near future for parties, clubs, and circle meetings, few of which she had ever attended when she had been well. The family members acted as though they were in complete control of every situation. And they were—except over the disease. They insisted that Mabel be given some drug or perhaps electric shock therapy so that she "wouldn't have to worry." They said they didn't want her "to be burdened." Under their relentless prodding, both the attending physician and Mabel agreed to shock therapy. When asked whether she would approve of such treatment, she told the therapist, "I guess I'll do anything to make my family comfortable." That had been the way she had always handled conflict.

Mabel's family exhibited hyper-independence characterized by attempts to control feelings for fear of showing their weaknesses. Unlike Dr. John, described in the example above, Mabel's family avoided frustration by refusing to look at illness or dying. Instead of focusing feelings of guilt or inadequacy on themselves, they blamed others. Mabel was made to adjust her feelings for their needs to the point that Mabel couldn't even identify her feelings. The family's sense of independence was exaggerated. No regulation of the hospital or procedure of care was left unchallenged. They brought friends to see Mabel, but if they became emotionally dependent in a way that they threatened the family's hyper-independence, the friends were rejected. Mabel's dying meant loss to them, but more significantly, their feelings of helplessness meant that their attempts to be independent were called into question. The family reacted with callous denial in their attempt to maintain a sense of autonomy.

Mabel related to her family's hyper-independence with over-dependent behavior. She avoided asking questions about her situation and responded to questions in ways she thought she was expected to answer. While her own dying was painful to her, her basic conflict was fear of rejection if she exhibited independent behavior or opinions.

Mrs. B

Mrs. B was a 45-year-old mother who became the frequent focus for comment by the hospital staff when she took up residency at the time her son was admitted. He was a patient in the acute care unit for leukemia patients. Mrs. B's husband showed some emotion about their son's condition, but never appeared to make any of the decisions concerning his treatment. Mrs. B was very demanding with the nurses, but when one of the male physicians or interns came into her son's room, she would quickly change her demeanor into that of a coquettish, helpless little girl. She tried to "baby" her 26-year-old son, saying such things as, "Now get well for Mommy, so Mommy can be happy again," or, "You are really making Mommy feel very tired keeping me at the hospital all of the time." At other times, she would blame her son's condition on her husband's neglect, the son's neglect, or their family physician, whom she now termed "an incompetent quack." She was never interested in the details of her son's illness or in any explanations of why he was not recovering. When it was obvious that her son was dying, she cried copiously—for herself, it seemed.

Mrs. B was very impulsive. Unlike Mabel, described in the example above, Mrs. B used her dependency as a means to control others. Self-indulgent, emotionally unstable, and over-reactive, she used hysterics to get her way. She seemed never to be able to develop mature, trusting relationships. In place of having a sense of confidence or a sense of responsibility, she always tried to seek out an ideal person, a father-figure who would protect her and who would solve all of her problems. She often used the means of seductiveness and helplessness to find such a person.

Because of her easy suggestibility, the hospital staff tried to minimize conflict by giving her few details of her son's illness. While they met her direct questions honestly, firmly, and patiently, they wisely avoided giving her elaborations. What statements the staff did make were exaggerated when used by Mrs. B in attempts to manipulate feelings of guilt or sympathy in people around her.

What her son's health crisis meant to her was revealed in her tantrum when he was pronounced dead. She jumped from her chair and rushed to his bedside screaming: "You have failed me! You have failed me! and I am very angry with you!" Not her son, but the means she had come to trust for handling crisis had failed her.

Mr. R

Mr. R was a 75-year-old man whose wife had been admitted to the hospital with heart congestion. She was also diagnosed as "senile." While Mr. R manifested some of the characteristics of senility himself, his hostile behavior was in keeping with what his relatives could recall about him as far back as they could remember. When approached by members of the hospital staff, by friends or relatives, he would accuse them of plotting against him and his wife. He appeared to everyone around him as self-centered, rigid, childish, and generally hostile. When he succeeded in driving most people away from him, he accused everybody of abandoning him in his hour of need, thereby confirming his most vivid suspicions about "this whole rotten world." Relatives were accused of coming to visit only to court favor for inheritance purposes. Physicians were accused of rendering no service but grabbing more money. Even his wife was failing him by dying first. Ridiculing and taunting, testing and reproving, he alienated himself from everyone, blaming them for what was missing in himself.

Hostility may take either active or passive forms. When active, people like Mr. R tend to explode emotionally as a standard reaction to new experiences and appear confirmed in the belief that they are victims of some conspiracy. When passive, they show their hostility in passive-aggressive pouting, stubbornness, or refusal to cooperate with care plans. Mr. R used hostility to try to prevent change until he could adjust—a painfully slow process for him. Now, with his deep feelings of loneliness, he was determined that he would be needed by his wife until she died. By driving most people away from his wife's room, he succeeded. But at the same time, his fears of having to continue living as a disgruntled, lonely old man were reinforced.

As a word of caution to the reader, it is important to distinguish between a person whose anger and hostility are characteristic of pre-aging personalities and a person who exhibits the symptoms as a result of age or disease. If hostility has not been part of his personality, it is then important to distinguish between organic and situational origins. Organic origins need to be determined by a physician. Most situational origins, such as bad care, failure to be listened to, or abandonment, can usually be corrected by demonstrated concern and affection.

Reducing Conflict

These six examples are intended to show how our perspective of the patient's health crisis and our expectations about the appropriate ways of handling emotional crises may be incompatible with other people's expectations and ways. When a physician handles his anxiety by trying to be efficient at the time relatives are ambiguous how to proceed with the patient's care; when a husband handles his anxiety by distancing himself emotionally just when his wife needs frequent affection for reassurance; when a patient handles his anxiety by verbalizing anger and hostility; when his relative handles anxiety by repressing emotions, conflict is the result.

For most of us—relatives, friends, staff, or patient—interpersonal conflict is more troublesome than the inner struggles we have with feelings of pain, grief, and ambiguity, now made particularly intense because "time is running out."

What can be done to reduce conflict? No one knows all that can be known about a patient's needs—not even a spouse of fifty years, or an eminent physician, or the patient himself. Consequently, it is important, for both the patient and us, that as broad a spectrum of perspectives as possible be available for designing a patient's care plan. That spectrum of perspectives should include family members, health care professionals, and the patient. It is the patient, however, who is the principal evaluator of what is appropriate or inappropriate care. It is his sense of dignity which is the plumb line by which our help must be judged; not *our* feelings, not *our* relationship with the patient, not *our* professional role.

When we begin to have interpersonal conflicts, we can do several things to reduce them.

First, we need to stop and ask ourselves what is behind our own feelings. Perhaps we have some feelings of guilt about our prior relationships with the patient. Perhaps we feel inadequate to meet our loved one's health crisis.

If so, a second thing we can do is ask for assistance for ourself, working through our own inner conflicts with someone sympathetic. Our clergyman, a social worker, a hospital chaplain, or a friend may be appropriate.

Third, we need to communicate with other members of the

family and the health care team, not in a combative or hostile way, but in ways that our own perspective can be of help in the planning for patient care. We have a right to know what we can expect from others and an obligation to find out what they expect of us.

Fourth, we need to be open to the variety of ways emotions are expressed in health crisis. Contrary to the way we may believe, and despite the way we may behave, our own emotional involvement with the patient usually prevents us from being very knowledgeable. On the one hand, we must rely on health care personnel for much of the knowledge needed in the patient's physical care precisely because they are not as emotionally involved. On the other hand, an expert's systematic application of knowledge may be neat and orderly and yet be utterly oppressive to the patient because it does not address the problem the patient *feels*. We need to address the patient at the level of his feelings.

Fifth, "love" for the patient should have our highest priority, even above some knowledgeable opinion, or concept of professional role, or sense of ethics. "Knowledge puffs up, but love builds up." Love even overcomes conflict.

5

When Dying Means Suffering

So teach us to number our days, that we may apply our hearts unto wisdom.

PSALM 90:12 KJV

"Why does man suffer?" Perhaps no other question has been wrestled with more persistently in human history than this one. The persistence and pervasiveness of suffering, however, has not kept us from believing that happiness should be normative for living. Suffering, we believe, ought not belong to life.

High expectations are placed on medical science. If, for some reason, suffering does occur, people expect the physician to prescribe a cure-all. But if not a cure-all, a pain "killer." Modern medicine has given us considerable control over many forms of pain, but it is not uncommon to discover that even when pain is relieved, suffering remains.

Loneliness, guilt, conflict—these and more are the elements of suffering. When suffering occurs, our natural inclination is to ask, "Why? Why me?" We question not only the phenomenon of the moment but the very nature of our existence.

Al was a 50-year-old white male from a blue collar suburb of Chicago. He was admitted to a metropolitan hospital after he was diagnosed with cancer of the liver. He was visited frequently by most members of his family and a few friends even though the hospital was far from home. Al's disease was inoperable, but he did not seem to be in great pain. Yet, despite the fact that staff and family were meeting his physical needs, he suffered greatly. He resisted talking about his feelings with his friends, but he was quite open with members of the health care staff. "Why?" he asked over and over. "Why should I be suffering?"

Occasions for Suffering

The question, "Why me?" indicates that a person is suffering because he believes his hopes and expectations are being violated. Al had never planned to suffer. He had been active at work and at home up until a month before his hospitalization. He had little warning of his health crisis. He was not prepared for any diagnosis as grave as the one he received. He was happily married and the father of two daughters and a son. He was active in the men's organization of his church. He enjoyed human contact with the people in his community. He and his wife, Erma, had worked hard but in doing so they were about to make the last payment on their house mortgage; they had been able to provide their children with more material goods than they themselves had in their youth; and they were well on the road to setting aside sufficient income for a comfortable retirement. The diagnosis of cancer simply was not in Al's plans.

When his physician shared the findings of the tests with him, Al's first reaction was disbelief. "Surely some mistake has been made." He became angry at the physician. "How could he do this to me?" Al sought an examination from a second physician, but the original diagnosis was confirmed. Still, Al couldn't believe "this is happening to me." "If the diagnosis is true," he thought, "all the careful planning that Erma and I have done is for nothing." Life had become meaningless.

Al suffered for another reason. While it was not the official teaching of his religion, he, like many of his friends, believed that disease is punishment for wrong-doing. Those who lived righteously, he believed, were rewarded with prosperity, good health, and longevity. When suffering occurred it was because the sufferer, or one of his relatives, had been immoral. And premature death was punishment for sins, overt or concealed, sometimes unknown even to those who commit them. How could he, a good man, now be suffering? The conflict violated his sense of logic and his notion of consistency.

Yet a third occasion for Al's suffering came as a consequence of the conflict between the person he thought he ought to be and the person who now felt so impotent. How was he to be the man he was supposed to be? The conflict offended his sense of propriety.

Occasions for Release from Suffering

Al struggled with his question, "Why me?" and in doing so began to reassess his expectations. He had always pictured himself as dying quickly—in an accident or from a heart attack. His family would mourn his death but there would be, in his mind's eye, no pain and no suffering. As he adapted to the realities of his illness, he seemed to give up being offended by the fact that his dying would be a lingering process. But this, in itself, brought no relief to his suffering.

Al found real comfort in the fact that his wife and daughters came to see him regularly. After one visit, he began to reminisce about the people and the things that were most important to him. He joked about his adventures in traveling all over the country when he was young and single, but it was his life as a father that he most treasured. When asked to name the things that were his most important achievements, his answers centered around the role of father. He had taught his girls to be modest; he had taught his son how to play ball and how to defend himself. He had taught them how to be honest and how to work hard.

His answers gave me the opportunity to ask, "And what do you have left to teach your son?" His son had never been mentioned except as Al reminisced about the boy's childhood.

Explosively, he reacted to my question: "What son! I don't have a son anymore!" Then he began to cry copiously.

After a while, Al began to speak again. "You know, I've talked about how the most important things in life to me have been in the things I've done as a father. But I've really failed as a father. My son won't let me teach him anything more. I kicked him out last year." Out poured a tale of painful conflict between a father and his teen-age son. "You ought to see him! He has hair down to his shoulders."

I asked him, "What is so important about the fact that your son has long hair?"

Incredulous, he asked a rhetorical question, "You know what long hair means in Cicero? It means my son isn't a man. I've failed to raise my son to be a man!" Long-hair styles for men became acceptable even in Cicero, but not at the time Al and his son were in conflict. It made little difference to Al that most of his son's friends also had long hair. And Al was little persuaded by understanding that his son would have been rejected by his peer group if he had the length of hair Al thought appropriate.

As their conflict stretched out into months, Al and his son were unable to communicate about anything. Their relationship was ruptured. Al interpreted his feelings as the occasion when his son "called the family's good name into question." Now embarrassment had become hard fact. Al understood himself not only to have failed as a father but as a son.

We didn't linger on the subject of hair very long, that wasn't the important point. I didn't want to miss the opportunity of calling him back to what he had articulated as the most important expectation he had for himself—the role of teacher. I asked my question again: "Is there something more that you can teach your son?"

Al thought for a while and then replied, "Well, I don't know what it could be."

"Is there such a thing as teaching him how to die well?" I asked. "Is there something about the experience that you're having now that would be valuable for him to know?"

Partial release from his suffering occurred as Al began to reflect on what he could yet give his son. He could use the occasion of his suffering to give his son a last gift.

In Al's desire for reconciliation with his son, he began to release his son as an object of anger. And as he discovered that he could forgive his son, Al began to have a change of heart about his notions of retribution. Some suffering, he could see, is the direct consequence of human error. Automobile accidents caused by drunken drivers, farm and industrial accidents that result from careless workers, an infant's injury which occurs while a mother is distracted, are all occasions of suffering as a direct consequence of human behavior. But what about cancer?

Al's physician explained that on the basis of medical research we know that most diseases are not the results of immoral or licentious behavior. In our attempts to find order in the chaos of our health crises, however, we easily draw cause-and-effect conclusions that have little or no bearing on reality. Some people try to explain their malignancies by postulating: "It was because of what happened to me when I was sixteen," or "I was hit there and became deeply bruised," or "I ate the wrong foods when I was a teen-ager," or again, "I sowed too many wild oats when I was a young-ster." Endless reasons can be given. Like many people, Al did not distinguish between those health crises that come as a direct result of human error and those that are from bodily breakdown.

By distinguishing between what he knew and what he could not know, Al gradually began to release himself from feelings of guilt based on the assumption that somehow, in some way unknown to him, his cancer was the consequence of grievous sins. He had been unwilling to verbalize it, but he feared that his cancer was God's punishment for having kicked his son out of the house. And he had wondered, too, if his son's errant behavior had brought divine disfavor down upon the family. In his anger, Al had been holding himself accountable for his disease, then his son, and finally God. Now he could be released from his notions of retribution.

Until Al had wrestled with the implications of forgiving and being forgiven, he thought he *ought* to be the perfect man. So long as he held to the pretense that he had to be a perfect, righteous man if he were to avoid punishment, he had held himself tenaciously to an accountability that neither he nor any other man is able to muster.

It was the Danish philosopher, Søren Kierkegaard, who reminded men of Al's persuasion that before God we are all failures, and therefore do not have to pretend a "sufferless-ness" none of us can attain. Al had believed that if he were anything less than perfect, he would be considered weak, impotent, and inadequate. This, he thought, would make him not only unacceptable to his family, but to God. Yet, secretly, he felt that he was a failure as a father and was about to be found out as his disease progressed. As Al was able to forgive his son and release him to be the man that the son was, Al was able to release himself to be the man that he truly was.

Al sent a letter to his son requesting that he come to the hospital as soon as possible. It was quite an emotional reconciliation. There were no words about hair. "I have lots to tell you," Al shared. "I need to tell you that I found out what it feels like to be cut off from someone you really love. I think it was more painful to me than this thing that's got me. I also want to give you something. I want to show you that you can still be a man even though you hurt. I want to show you that you can die without being destroyed."

Al died soon after reconciling himself with his son. It was a peaceful death. Like the biblical Job, Al suffered because of the conflict he felt between his expectations for himself and the reality of his health crisis. Ironically, his sense of worth was restored when he discovered that he had not been rejected because he was an imperfect man. He was released from alienation when his loneliness was pierced in the sharing of love with another. His release came not as a result of any good works, but in the awareness that he was accepted even though, in his words, he no longer "worked good."

Occasions for Addressing Suffering Therapeutically

Release from the offense of suffering comes when a person discovers "in the defenselessness of suffering the dissolution of defensiveness." [7] There probably is not one among us who has the insight or ability to avoid occasions for suffering. I do not say that suffering is necessary. But occasions of suffering are a part of life and do force us to reexamine our expectations for life. They also force on us the discovery of our pretensions. When one we love is critically or terminally ill, we suffer. His pain stimulates our suffering. We may try terribly hard to pretend that we aren't threatened, that we can be strong enough to meet his every need, that we can be the perfect companion in crisis. But if the truth be told, one of the occasions for a patient's suffering is seeing how his crisis causes us pain, and the more we pretend that this is not so, the more defensive we become and the more susceptible we are to reacting with what I have described as the Abandonment Syndrome or the Surrogate Suffering Syndrome.

Part of our defensiveness is expressed when we refuse to talk with the patient about his suffering. In an attempt to "do the right thing" relatives sometimes request that the patient not even be told the nature of his crisis.

Marian tried to be a "surrogate sufferer" for her mother. Marian was a smartly dressed, middle-aged woman. When the diagnostic results became available, she instructed the physician not to tell her mother. The physician wrote the following order on the patient's chart: "Do not inform patient of either her diagnosis or prognosis." In the following days, the patient wondered why no one was saying anything to her about the very reason for which she had come to the hospital. Marian would make bright, guarded conversation as she hovered protectively at bedside, and physicians and nurses evaded her questions.

Why had Marian insisted that her mother not be informed about her incurable disease? "My mother is a very good woman. She has had to put up with a lot of suffering in her life, most of it inflicted by other people. I'm not going to let her suffer any more." Ironically, the daughter was reenacting an episode of suffering inflicted on her mother by other people.

I have never informed a patient that he is dying. I have never needed to do so. Patients come to a hospital for a reason. They have suspicions, fears, and feelings about being there. If possible, most patients like to leave a hospital as soon as possible with the hope that they can carry on a normal life. The longer they are held in the hospital, the greater the suspicions, fears, and feelings about being there. I suppose there are patients who have been hoodwinked by relatives and staff; but I have yet to meet one. Evasion is a lie, and once you tell a lie, you have to build a care plan around it. Too many people are involved with administering a patient's care plan to maintain effective deceptiveness. Consequently, relatives and physicians who try to keep a diagnosis from a patient usually are frustrated. But not in the way popularly thought.

At the University of Chicago I began a study to see how patients who have not been told their diagnosis nevertheless seemed to know that they had a grim prognosis. Out of a sample of 65 patients, I found the following results. All but one of the terminally ill patients told me that they thought they were dying. The one exception had become comatose before I could complete the study.

I would ask the patient, "Why are you here?"

Some patients would first test me to see how I would react to their feelings. That was the way it was with Marian's mother. Then, guardedly, she said, "Well, I think I have cancer. And I'm going to die from it."

"How do you know this?" I asked.

"I don't think I'm suppose to know. My daughter sees to that. But I know. Everyone started acting funny the day I was suppose to hear what is wrong."

Another patient identified the very person who had given

the order not to tell as the one who had, in fact, communicated the news to her: "My doctor has always looked me squarely in the eyes when talking to me—until that day. He has not looked at my face since completing his work-up of my case. I know the results even though he told me I was going to be fine."

In more than 80 percent of the cases, ironically, the person who had ordered that the diagnosis be kept secret was the one whom the patient identified as having revealed the secret.

Various communication studies indicate that we convey less than 30 percent of our feelings by words. Over 70 percent of our feelings are conveyed through gestures. Patients know relatives and staff better than we know the patient. All of the patient's attention can be focused on our behavior. We usually have other concerns, particularly when we try to keep a secret. So the question is not, "Should we tell the patient?" But, "What is the best way to communicate the diagnosis?"

The attempt to shoulder a patient's suffering for him is as futile as to try to do his dying for him. Every attempt to be the surrogate sufferer imposes an additional burden of suffering on him.

We err when we think that what our loved one most needs from us is to be perfect, unsuffering, and unfeeling. As one woman put it, "It would be so nice if I could just talk with my husband and children about our common suffering. But we can't. If I indicate that I am suffering, they begin to twitch as though I'm accusing them of neglect. They think they have to be so brave and strong. But the more helpless they really feel, the most pushy they become. That's why I like talking to you. You're nobody to me. I can say what I really feel like saying without fearing unwanted consequences. Still, it would really be a comfort if I could share my feelings with those I love."

Just as patients need someone to help them work through their feelings in order to be released from their questions of self-pity and anger, so we need help discovering the origins of our feelings. As we try to do "the right thing" for the patient, as we try to be the perfect companion, we force ourselves into giving the patient pretentiousness when he needs compassion. Who but one who has suffered can know the *meaning* of compassion?

"Why does man suffer?" Because we are mortals. And all schemes for avoiding or eliminating suffering are soon exposed as pious deceits when we, ourselves, suffer. We do not will to suffer. But man's suffering is the sole source of his understanding and insight into the afflictions of others. Suffering can curse our life with bitterness and resentment, but it can also enable us to reach out in sympathetic concern toward another who suffers. The suffering we have in common, then, can be the occasion for a healing relationship of love and acceptance. It is the answer to our prayer "that we may apply our hearts unto wisdom."

6

When Dying Means Triumph

O death, where is thy victory?
O death, where is thy sting?

1 COR. 15:55 RSV

How can dying ever mean triumph?

When I began my career nearly 15 years ago, it never occurred to me that I could write such a chapter as this. The reason I am able to do so is because of the insights shared by my many teachers—more than 600 critically and terminally ill patients, their families, and the health care personnel who served them. Before learning from them, I was skeptical that dying could mean anything other than the "horrific," "final tragedy," which "ends everything worthwhile." Either that, or, for life to have meaning, death had to be an illusion.

Dying did mean "the end of everything worthwhile" to some patients, and other patients so feared death that they tried desperately to believe that life is unending. *Dying can be terribly threatening.* One woman was quite correct when she warned that it would only be another game of rationalization if we tried "to domesticate death."

For most of us, "death" and "dying" are such generalized concepts that we do not know what generates our fears. Not unlike children who are afraid of the dark because they can't focus on the unexperienced, many of us fear dying as an unknown. Given the time to work through their feelings, the overwhelming majority of patients found that they not only could, but did, conquer their fears. While failing to domesticate death, they nevertheless could measure their dying against living rather than living in fear of dying. The overwhelming majority of patients found that they could both affirm their life and acknowledge the realities of their dying. Released from conflict, they could live—and die—in dignity.

What Power Has Death?

Initially, almost all patients had fears that they could not cope with dying. They had to struggle to put their experience in a perspective they could grasp. "I just didn't expect it to be this way," one man confessed. Patients had to discover if their expectations, beliefs, and values would betray them in their hour of crisis. More importantly, they had to discover whether dying would cut them off from the love that had made life worth living.

Some patients discovered that rather than trusting the Lord whom they had named in their prayers, they had been obedient through fear to the god, Death. Some patients discovered that they were so burdened by inherited, corporate guilt, they had been persuaded that death is the ultimate moral power in their lives: "death befalls the wicked" is the commandment of Death. Some patients discovered that their sense of righteousness was not based on some sharing of love with another or on their sense of morality but on a belief that their behavior was an insurance policy against insecurity, suffering, and loneliness. They discovered that they had given much of their lives in unwitting appeasement to Death.

Western anthropologists seem to relish being able to identify the taboos of primitive people as though somehow taboos are characteristic of primitives. But many patients discovered that those of us in the "civilized" West also have taboos, for example, the never questioned but obediently served fears of dying. Their fears had shaped their emotions, their behavior, their outlook on life. Like the sting of a farmer's electric fence that keeps cows corralled, these fears had kept them imprisoned. This is Death's power.

The power of Death comes from irrational fears that drive us to pretend that "loss" is not inherent in living, that "suffering" is not appropriate for the righteous, that "conflict" is immoral for the loving—a life not one of us can attain. If we have committed ourselves to a life-style of avoidance, dying then can be the most anxiety producing experience of our living. This is Death's sting. Death has defined our life.

Our Puritan fathers knew well the power of Death. In the wilderness of New England they were committed to building a "city on a hill" that could be used as an example of God's will for men around the world. Yet, in their wisdom, even as they proclaimed their allegiance to God—called Jehovah or YHWH by some—the Puritans knew how easily they could be seduced into service to Death. Included in their catechism was the question: "If it be the will of the Lord, are you willing to be damned for his glory?" The great commandment of God is: "You shall love the Lord your God with all your heart, and with all your soul, and with all your mind." [8] If a Puritan were not able to answer the catechetical question with, "yes," he knew his true allegiance was other than to God. The question reminded him that simply to proclaim one's obedience does not mean that one has given his heart.

Many patients wrestled with the question of allegiances. They saw their struggles as a re-enactment, for them, of the cosmological battle between Good and Evil, between the God of Life and the power of Death. Some patients spoke of struggling with the devil; others, with suffering. But regardless of how they identified their conflict, they wrestled with basic questions about human nature.

When we look at ancient Egypt, we see how concerned the pharaohs were with their own struggles against death. The pharaohs considered themselves, by nature, privileged and quite unlike the mortals over whom they ruled. They thought of themselves as gods, and therefore, immortal by definition. Their preparations for protecting themselves against death were most impressive. Yet, as monumental as the pyramids are, they stand as revelations of the extremes to which human beings can go in desperate attempts to sand bag our lives against the power of Death.

In ancient Greece, the gods of Olympus were believed to have all of the characteristics of common men except one— immortality. When a common mortal died, it was forever. When one of the gods was "killed," it was only for a time. An artifact from 400 B.C. shows one of the gods giving a grand feast for all of his divine friends who had mourned his "death" in a game. Now the game was over.

As civilization emerged, the Greeks took for themselves the characteristics they ascribed to their gods. But only "citizens," few in number, could have these characteristics. The barbarians, the non-citizens of Greek culture, remained very mortal. Plato was a citizen, not a barbarian, and his philosophy of the soul, which has had so much influence on Western thought, reflected the notion that man, at least as a soul, has the potential of being as immortal as a god. Despite Plato's wisdom, his thought was not widely accepted for many generations after his death.

By the time of the Common Era, many peoples in the Mediterranean region, including the ruling Romans, believed that the god Death was the most powerful deity. Even some of the Semites believed Death had ultimate power.

A small group of Hebrews were convinced that while Death was very powerful, he was not supreme. When one of them, Jesus of Nazareth believed by the Romans to be spreading sedition, was crucified at Calvary, the event was seen as the final dethronement of Death. According to their account, even though Jesus was crucified, dead, and buried, on the third day, he was raised up from the dead by God. This event revealed that even Death is subject to the God of Life. For those who saw the event as release from the power of Death, life became new. It was a resurrection for them, too. These people saw men's attempts to be perfect—to ascribe to themselves the characteristics of God—as the sin of pride which, rather than preserving life, cuts men off from the Source of life.

When Christianity became politically acceptable throughout the Mediterranean region, the old Greek idea of man's perfectibility and the ideal for striving for immortality still found many believers. They accommodated their beliefs to the new religion by teaching the injunction: "Be perfect, like Jesus," and by proclaiming that Jesus had become so perfect in nature, he had raised himself up from the dead, thereby indicating that all men can become immortal if we will but do, think, or feel the right things. The struggle between the Greek and the Hebrew visions of human nature still exists, and many patients discovered that their emotional conflicts were an embodiment of contradictory and competing claims for allegiance. Like the questions of the Puritan fathers, the patient's question, "If it be the will of the Lord, am I willing to die for his glory?" was not only instructive, but self-revelatory. And in that revelation, many of the patients felt relieved—and triumphant.

But What Ending for Life?

As relieved as some patients were in being released from their conflicts, they sensed that there was still the possibility of losing their victory. As in Bunyan's *The Pilgrim's Progress,* hell is never closer than at heaven's door. John Bunyan wrote his allegory about man's struggles with living. The Pilgrim's road, he thought, is mined with traps, temptations, and terrors, any one of which could destroy one's hopes for destiny. Even before the gates of heaven, there is a final test—a trap door that opens directly into hell.

You may think that Bunyan's vocabulary is antiquated. Perhaps you don't use the words, "heaven" or "hell." Many of the patients in our research group didn't either. Some of them disavowed any belief in "afterlife," "eternity," "heaven," or "hell." Nevertheless, they were still concerned about how life would end. They were concerned that they would end with a sense of purpose completed, of destiny. Whatever the choice of vocabulary, basic to the concept of "heaven" is the meaning of life fulfilled or completed. Basic to the concept of "hell" is the sense that life is incomplete, finished, or alienated.

Some patients, particularly those who were in intensive care units or who had survived traumatic kinds of accidents, reported that before their conditions had stabilized, all they could think about was the horror that their life was being cut off. "This just can't be happening to me," one girl kept saying to herself, "I'm too young!" She reported that she was shocked by the unexpected accident, but she was horrified by the memories of "all the terrible times of my life. My life seemed so meaningless. It was just hell!"

Other accident victims reported that even though they knew they were dying, they felt no fear or horror. In recorded testimony, some Swiss ski-accident survivors, who thought they were dying, reported that beautiful memories of their lives passed through their minds as they were falling. Their only anxiety was what they saw registered on the faces of their rescuers.[9]

Age seems to have some effect on the interpretation a person has of his end. Some young or middle-aged patients expressed deep anger about their life being "cut short." Many older patients not only thought death was appropriate but looked forward to the relief it would bring. In a recent study conducted for the National Institute of Mental Health, 55 percent of the old people *in good health* seemed to have resolved their struggles with death, 30 percent manifested denial, and 15 percent expressed alarm.

Mrs. P. was one of those who had already resolved her struggle with dying. A 66-year-old former school teacher, she had been born and reared in a "religious" family. She had married a man from a similar background and together they lived out what she called "a quest for value." Mrs. P. was widowed at age 40. She finished the rearing of their two daughters, who were now married with families of their own, and she retired from her career.

Mrs. P. was confined to the hospital for the last four weeks of her life. Like many terminal patients, she had a sense of timing about the approach of her end. Friends were requested to come to the hospital, and without being either morbid or lengthy, she spoke to each in turn on what they had meant to her. She had written out instructions for her daughters about the disposition of her belongings and the kind of disposal she preferred for her body. When friends were uneasy in her presence or tried to play games about the reality of the situation, she very calmly, yet strongly, assured them: "We don't have to be afraid. Parting is difficult so let's cry together for a little while; then we can talk." And that is what they would do. Several days before she died, she called together each daughter with her family and celebrated their reunion. Her business done, she asked an old and dear friend to be with her until the end. As she grew weaker, there was less and less conversation, but words were not necessary. She died in the manner for which she prepared—at peace.

It is doubtful that anyone could have broken Mrs. P's spirits. She was too disciplined and experienced in her faith. But for those who have not had her experience, even though they may sense victory over their fears of dying, they can be entrapped by the panic and alienation felt by those around them. Emma is an example.

Emma was elderly. She was also very bitter. She had been resuscitated following a cardiac arrest. "I remember going to sleep. It was so peaceful. Then there was this terrible intrusion, like an alarm clock going off in my ear. I've always hated alarm clocks; I would think I was having a heart attack they startled me so. That was what it was like when the doctor brought me back, only more so, and I can remember thinking, 'Who is this intruder?' I shall never forgive him. Never!"

It was very hard for the physician to understand why Emma was not grateful to him for "saving her life." In the conflict between them is revealed the difference between a life ending "alienated" and a life ended "fulfilled." When we understand that the meaning a patient gives to life may be far more valuable than preservation of vital signs, we can serve *the patient* rather than our own fears. Emma had "completed" her life, only to be called back. "For what purpose?" she kept demanding. As in Bunyan's allegory, at the very gates of heaven, Emma was pushed through a trapdoor of chaos into a state of alienated hell by an overly anxious physician.

Jack's life could have ended like Emma's, but it didn't.

Jack was a young, husky, and handsome truck driver who was mangled in a highway accident and arrived conscious at the emergency room. Appearing to struggle for survival with every ounce of energy he could muster, his spirit inspired the emergency room staff to the limits of their talents. The sounds of the brisk orders, the rustle of the staff's rapid movements, the whining of the emergency equipment seemed to stimulate his adrenalin even more. But his injuries were too severe. The staff's frantic last efforts could have panicked him had it not been for the comforting words of the sister who made the emergency room her arena for ministry. Leaning close to his ear, she called him by name and said, "You're in good hands, Jack." Barely audible, his last words were, "Thank you for reminding me, sister."

Life "completed" is life related, invested with love, and full of meaning. Whatever a patient's age, whatever the patient's crisis, love unsevered by dying is living in triumph.

Given time to work through crisis, a patient can cope with even the most frightening of experiences. None seems to be any more frightening than the thoughts of bleeding to death. Yet when artery walls weaken, some patients know that their end will come that way. Mr. G, in his middle sixties, became aware of a strange bulge in his neck after he had lifted a bale of hay onto his wagon. The bulge is called an aneurysm. When he was told by physicians that there was nothing that they could do surgically to correct his condition, his anxieties became more and more acute. Family physicians and nurses were beside themselves empathizing with the man's terror.

The student nurse assigned to him spent considerable time sharing mutual concerns about the world. She could begin to sense the things that were important to him, what his styles of living had been, what his ideals were. Of German background, he and his wife kept a meticulously clean house. His machinery and tools were kept in the best of condition. He had always been careful about his personal appearance. Talking with the student nurse, he revealed his anxiety: he was afraid, despite his faith, that he would die "in a mess." Since he was able to focus on his concern, with the help of his family and the health care staff he could prepare to cope accordingly. He asked the nurses what they expected to do when the aneursym broke, and they showed him a stack of towelling. He spent most of an afternoon reorganizing the towelling, moving it closer to his chair, with the corner of the top towel turned up so that it could be easily grabbed.

On the student nurse's graduation day, she came to tell Mr. G good-bye. They relived together their many conversations and rehearsed their preparation for what he called "his graduation." As the young nurse rose to leave, the moment they both anticipated happened. Calmly, confidently, the patient grabbed the top towel and pressed it against his neck. He thanked the young nurse for all her help: "You have earned your degree." Those were the last words he spoke. Because he was able to cope with his fears of dying, he was able to end his life as he had prepared.

Any patient can be thwarted in his attempt to complete that end which he desires, and many are. Sometimes he is thwarted by life-long patterns of uncertainty and avoidance; sometimes he is frustrated with a weak sense of identity. But sometimes he is panicked by the behavior of overly anxious relatives and health-care staff. Our task is to support our loved one in his attempts to resolve the conflicts of his crisis even when we ourselves feel helpless, in conflict, or hopeless. It may be that if we allow ourselves to be instructed by the dying, we ourselves will be relieved from that which binds us to Death.

What Meaning Has "Triumph"?

One of the hardest things for me to learn from critically and terminally ill patients was that my own feelings of anxiety blinded me from sharing their perceptions. Often the perceptions of the patients are in sharp contrast to the interpretations of the onlookers. Yet, when I was able to grant to a patient his own perceptions, I was able to discover how dying can mean triumph. To overcome fears that have tyrannized living, to conquer doubts that love can prevail, to discover who "I am," was a victory of great prize for almost all patients.

Something strange and beautiful often happened when a patient came to the end of life. All fear, all horror seemed to disappear. "I have often watched a look of happy wonder dawn in his eyes when he realized what was happening," writes a veteran nurse. "He seemed to come alive in a new form." I concur.

As patients no longer had to live with pretense about their nature, when they gave up plotting and calculating how to preserve their lives, when they no longer had to avoid dying because of their fears of death—then, ironically, the meaning of living took on the characteristics of new life. Sometimes tranquilly, sometimes with a smile, other times with bursts of joy, patients expressed relief in the destruction of their last enemy. They were no longer subjects of Death. What time there was to live—and for some it was only a moment—they could now love the gift of life that had been given them. It was the time, "when the perishable puts on the imperishable, and the mortal puts on immortality." For the time has come when they could confess: "Death is swallowed up in victory. O death, where is thy victory? O death, where is thy sting?"

Death dethroned! This is the meaning of dying in triumph. It is a lesson which has been shared from the death bed for generations. It is shared now by those who, in many instances, were making their last gift, given for those of us who have yet to experience. It won't be easy, it won't be without great struggle, but for those of us who mourn, to know that dying need not cut us off from the Love which has made living worthwhile is the most comforting reassurance I can imagine.

Notes

1. Sr. Mary Catherine O'Conner. *The Art of Dying Well* (New York: Columbia University Press, 1942), p. 4.
2. Matthew 6:21 RSV.
3. I am indebted to the research of Humberto Nagera and associates for the section on the meaning of loss for children. See his "Children's Reactions to the Death of Important Objects," *Psychoanalytic Study of the Child*, Vol. 25 (1970), pp. 360-400.
4. From the research of Anna Freud and H. Hartmann, cited by H. Nagera.
5. John Bowlby and C. Murray Parkes, "Separation and Loss Within the Family," in E. James Anthony and Cyrille Koupernik, *The Child in His Family.* (New York: John Wiley & Sons, 1970), pp. 197-198.
6. Other metaphors have been used by my former colleagues. Elisabeth Kübler-Ross used the metaphor, "stage," to describe a patient's characteristic behavior based on early findings of the Chicago "Program on Death and Dying." See her *On Death and Dying* (New York: Macmillan Company, 1969). The late Carl Nighswonger used the metaphor, "drama." See his "Ministry to the Dying as a Learning Encounter," *Journal of Thanatology*, Vol. 1, No. 2 (March-April 1971).

97

7. M. Holmes Hartshorne, "The Grace of Suffering," a sermon preached in the Colgate University Chapel, May 3, 1964.
8. Matthew 22:37 RSV.
9. Russell Noyes, Jr., "The Experience of Dying," *Psychiatry*, Vol. 35 (May 1972).

APPENDIX

Some Models for Mourners

Suggested Further Reading

Some Models for Mourners

Grief is the normal reaction to death of a loved one, whether the death was sudden or anticipated. It is characterized by inner questioning, depressed moods, restlessness, loss of interest in the affairs of others, sleep disturbance, loss of appetite, or weight loss. If the hurts of the bereaved are to heal, normal reaction should also include ventilation of emotions, such as crying.

The common mistake of mourners is attempting to hide their grief, to try processing their feelings by themselves. Solitude is appropriate at times, but feelings of loss are easily transformed into loneliness, and loneliness is easily translated into feelings of alienation. The more lonely the mourner becomes, the less likely he will find healthy release from his sorrow.

If you are a mourner, several of the following models of assistance may help you handle your grief in a healthier manner.

One-to-One Counseling

Sometimes we try to "bottle up" our emotions by maintaining the pretense that nothing has happened when we have lost someone very dear to us. The very fact that we are bereaved is evidence that something basic has happened and to maintain the pretense adds to the burden of our sorrow. It also adds to our health hazards.

Even for those mourners who express their grief openly, the presence of a sympathetic listener helps the process of adapting to loss. Clergymen, social workers, and psychiatric nurses, funeral directors, lawyers, and trust officers, even sympathetic laypersons can be effective in assisting the mourner make decisions, confirm and assess his loss, regain perspective, establish new priorities for living, and discover new interests. The basic need is for someone who can listen sympathetically without being threatened by the mourner's ventilation of emotions or exaggeration of feelings. It is being able "to share my innermost feelings without having to worry about consequences," as one widow put it.

While one-to-one counseling is an effective model for initial processing of grief, it ought not be used exclusively. The goal for individual counseling ought to be assisting the mourner to function more effectively in a social context. If individual counseling is sustained, it can deteriorate into unnecessary and untherapeutic dependencies.

Make Today Count

Founded by Orville Kelly, an Iowa newsman with cancer, "Make Today Count" (MTC) is an organization that helps cancer patients cope openly with their feelings and assists them in relating better to the mourning of their loved ones. The motto for the program is: "Don't think of the future. Just get the most out of each minute of each day."

The people who wrestle most effectively with reactions to cancer are cancer patients who know how to tap their own emotional resources and who are willing to share with others. The chapters of MTC are designed less for exchanges of agonies, however, than for matter-of-fact sharing about problem solving. MTC encourages cancer patients to communicate with one another, in group meetings if possible, or by telephone. For more information about the work of MTC, write: Mr. Orville Kelly, 218 S. 6th Street, Burlington, Iowa 52601.

National Foundation for Sudden Infant Death

Local chapters of the National Foundation for Sudden Infant Death have a two-fold purpose: 1) to support research of Sudden Infant Death Syndrome (SIDS), and 2) to assist families who may be suffering needless guilt based on uninformed notions about the disease.

SIDS strikes between two and three babies out of every one thousand births and accounts for 85% of unexpected infant deaths. It can neither be predicted nor prevented, even by a physician. The Old Testament referred to SIDS as "overlaying" (1 Kings 3:19). Folklore calls it "crib" or "cot death" and usually attributes it to suffocation. Apparently because of a nearly instantaneous death, there is sometimes spasm, which leads the discovering parent to assume that the infant has been suffocated by bed clothes, has aspirated on regurgitated food, or has been maltreated.

Parents suffer not only from the shock of their infant's unexpected death but from the erroneous suspicions of relatives, policemen, coroners, and others, who jump to the conclusion that malicious neglect is self-evident. Every year young couples have been jailed by vindictive officials who fail to distinguish between victims of SIDS and perpetrators of child abuse, thus making the suffering of the parents all the more acute.

Local SIDS chapters attempt to educate public officials about the nature of the disease, intervene on behalf of stricken parents as quickly as possible, and refer parents to competent counselors. Most SIDS chapters are not designed to give professional counseling services.

As a model for mourners, these organizations fill the needs for on-the-spot and prompt intervention that both shields the mourners while they are in the depths of shock and assists them in getting competent assistance. Studies at the University of Washington show that parents of SIDS victims tend to be far more depressed than parents of children who die of better known diseases and whose deaths were anticipated. The same studies also demonstrate the need for giving assistance to siblings who may feel guilty because of normal feelings of ambivalence about loss of their younger rival.

For further information, write: National Foundation for Sudden Infant Death, 1501 Broadway, New York, New York 10036.

Widow-to-widow and Widower Programs

If one-to-one counseling is appropriate for helping the individual mourner in the initial period of grief or when he is having difficulty resolving conflicts of loss, programs like "widow-to-widow" and "widower" groups are appropriate for helping the mourner become reoriented to a social context.

A mourner may protest, "But I don't want anyone else to know how much I hurt," or "I don't need to hear anyone else's problems; I have enough of my own." In doing so, he reveals not the need for solitude but the fear that he will be rejected because of his grieving. A number of sorrowing relatives and friends report that after the death of their loved one, they knew how important it was to ventilate emotions and work through feelings of conflict, but when they tried to do so, it embarrassed the people around them. "Now I know what Fred went through when he tried to talk to us about dying," one widow confessed. Groups of people coming together at times of need can provide a social context for healing that may not otherwise be available to the mourner. In a group, mourners can look at common problems, get experienced assistance in assessing feelings of loss, find morale support in working out solutions to problems, and as important as any of the above, share in turn with others who have been hurt by loss of a loved one.

Widowers, in particular, may need assistance reorienting themselves to social contexts. A study by the National Center for Health Statistics indicates that the death rate for America's two million widowers is double that of married men in comparable age categories above the age of 45. For white widowers between the ages of 20 and 34, the death rate is the highest for any segment of the male population. Major causes of death for them are vascular diseases, lung and stomach cancers, cirrhosis of the liver, and arteriosclerotic heart disease, indicating direct and indirect connections between incomplete or inadequate mourning and physical and mental breakdown.

Some churches, associations of funeral directors, and mental health associations have organized groups for mourners. Call your pastor or local hospital social service office to find the nearest group available for you. For assistance with organizing a group, write: Widows Consultation Center, 136 E. 57 St., New York, N.Y. 10022.

Parents Without Partners

For some mourners, feelings of grief must compete with the responsibilities of raising dependent children. Parents Without Partners, Inc., with chapters across the country, provides crisis intervention centers, research, and public education programs on the problems for single parents, referral services for various agencies that have special competencies for working with children, and educational and social programs for parents and their children. The goals of the organization focus on endeavors to bring children to healthy maturity, and to overcome the problems of being an isolated parent in society. International headquarters are located at 7910 Woodmont Avenue, Washington, D.C. 20014.

Preventive Therapy for Mourners

We really know very little about "anticipatory grief." The term in recent years has come to mean separation anxieties that occur as a person anticipates the loss of someone very dear.

Several research and training centers have begun systematic study of preventive therapy for persons who anticipate major loss: children, spouses, and friends. For example, when a mother of three preteenage children was diagnosed with spreading cancer, she encouraged her husband and children to begin receiving the kind of psychosocial support she was receiving. The therapy helped her husband to be far more supportive of her needs and helped him better understand his own feelings. The therapy was particularly effective for the children. They were encouraged to ask questions and to talk about their feelings which were stimulated by their mother's illness and hospitalization. After her death the children's period of mourning seemed considerably shorter and less severe than for children who had received no assistance.

If you anticipate a period of mourning, consult your pastor or counselor to identify resources that may help you respect your emotional needs when the brunt of crisis confronts you.

Suggested Further Reading

ON ETHICS AND THE DYING
Nelson, James B. *Human Medicine: Ethical Perspectives on New Medical Issues.* Minneapolis: Augsburg Publishing House, 1973.

ON GRIEF, MOURNING, AND BEREAVEMENT
Gorer, Geoffrey. *Death, Grief, and Mourning.* Garden City, N.Y.: Doubleday & Co., 1967.

Schoenberg, Bernard, ed., *Anticipatory Grief.* New York: Columbia University Press, 1974.

———— ed., *Loss and Grief.* New York: Columbia University Press, 1970.

Switzer, David K. *The Dynamics of Grief: Its Source, Pain, and Healing.* Nashville: Abingdon Press, 1970.

ON HELPING CHILDREN
Grollman, Earl A., ed., *Explaining Death to Children.* Boston: Beacon Press, 1967.

————, ed. *Talking About Death: A Dialogue Between Parent and Child.* Illustrated by Gisela Heau. Boston: Beacon Press, 1970.

Jackson, Edgar N. *Telling a Child About Death*. New York: Channel Press, 1965.

Stein, Sara Bonnett. *About Dying: An Open Family Book for Parents and Children Together*. Photography by Dick Frank. New York: Walker and Company, 1974.

ON THE HISTORY OF THE IDEA OF DEATH

Choron, Jacques. *Death and Western Thought*. New York: Colliers Books, 1963.

Mills, Liston O., ed. *Perspectives on Death*. Nashville: Abingdon Press, 1969. Includes essays by Lou H. Silberman, "Death in the Hebrew Bible and Apocalyptic Literature"; Leander E. Keck, "New Testament Views of Death"; and Milton McC. Gatch, "Some Theological Reflections on Death from the Early Church Through the Reformation."

Stendahl, Krister, ed. *Immortality and Resurrection*. New York: The Macmillan Company, 1965.

Toynbee, Arnold, ed. *Man's Concern with Death*. New York: McGraw-Hill Book Company, 1968.

ON THE PSYCHOLOGY OF DYING AND DEATH

Choron, Jacques. *Death and Modern Man*. New York: Colliers Books, 1964.

Herzong, Edgar. *Psyche and Death*. New York: G. P. Putnam's Sons, 1967.

Kastenbaum, Robert & Ruth Aisenberg. *The Psychology of Death*. New York: Springer Publishing Company, Inc., 1972.

Neale, Robert E. *The Art of Dying*. New York: Harper & Row, Publishers, 1973.

ON THE SOCIOLOGY OF DYING AND DEATH

Dumont, Richard G., and Dennis C. Foss. *The American View of Death: Acceptance or Denial?* Cambridge, Mass.: Schenkman Publishing Company, Inc., 1972.

Fulton, Robert, ed. *Death & Identity.* New York: John Wiley & Sons., Inc., 1965.

Sudnow, David. *Passing On: The Social Organization of Dying.* Englewood Cliffs, N.J.: Prentice-Hall, Inc., 1967.

FOR THE THOROUGH READER

Fulton, Robert, ed. *A Bibliography on Death, Grief and Bereavement 1845-1973.* Third Revised Edition. Minneapolis: University of Minnesota Center for Death Education and Research, 1973.

Other Titles in the
Religion and Medicine Series

GLEN W. DAVIDSON, EDITOR

UNDERSTANDING MENTAL ILLNESS: A LAY-MAN'S GUIDE

A book to help you understand the types of mental illness and their symptoms, professional therapy and how you can help, and the relationship of religion to mental health. *By Nancy C. Andreasen, Ph.D., M.D., assistant professor of psychiatry at the University of Iowa College of Medicine.*

WHAT CAN I DO ABOUT THE PART OF ME I DON'T LIKE?

"The part of me I don't like" may be a birth defect, physical handicap, speech problem, or a disabling disease. David Belgum helps you understand these personal problems and shows how you can accept and overcome them. *By David R. Belgum, Ph.D., member of the faculties of the School of Religion and the College of Medicine of the University of Iowa.*

HELPING YOUR HANDICAPPED CHILD

A handicapped child can lead a significant and valuable life. This book shows how parents can meet the child's needs, use community resources, and gain strength through faith. *By George Paterson, Ph.D. in pastoral counseling, who is on the staff of University Hospitals at the University of Iowa.*